The Bible Tells Them So

The Bible Tells Them So
The Discourse of Protestant Fundamentalism

Kathleen C. Boone

State University of New York Press

Published by
State University of New York Press, Albany

© 1989 State University of New York

For information, address State University of New York
Press, State University Plaza, Albany, N.Y. 12246

Library of Congress Cataloging in Publication Data

Boone, Kathleen C., 1957–
    The Bible tells them so : the discourse of Protestant
fundamentalism / Kathleen C. Boone.
        p.   cm.
    Bibliography: p. 129
    Includes index.
    ISBN 0–88706–894–4. ISBN 0–88706–895–2 (pbk.)
    1. Fundamentalism — Controversial literature. 2. Bible — Evidences,
authority, etc. 3. Bible — Criticism, interpretation, etc.
I. Title.
BT82.2.B66 1988
230'.044 — dc19   88–7270
                                                                CIP

10 9 8 7 6 5 4 3 2 1

For Blair

Contents

Preface

When Protestant fundamentalists defend any belief — whether religious, moral, or political — they invariably contend that the belief is "biblical." They believe what they believe because the Bible tells them so. While Bible believers pride themselves on their fidelity to the Word of God, it is that same singular devotion to the Word which draws the harshest criticism from outsiders. Fundamentalists have been accused of "hiding behind the Bible," cynically manipulating a sacred text to garner divine sanction for their hidden private and public agenda.

I am convinced, however, that most fundamentalists are sincere in their Bible belief. The popular image of the fundamentalist — the smug television preacher who inveighs against the immorality of "secular humanists" while fulfilling his own lusts in secret — is an anomaly. For every such figure, there are millions of other fundamentalists, less visible and therefore less notorious. The scholar grappling with difficult biblical texts, attempting to reconcile the mercy of God with the existence of hell. The modestly dressed woman from the local fundamentalist church who appears on our porch one day to ask shyly, "Do you know Jesus Christ as your personal Savior?" The grim young boy who carries his Bible to class in a private Christian school, where he learns that he is different from the other neighborhood boys, that he is "saved" and that he has a moral duty to share the gospel with everyone he meets. Each of these disparate figures is a Bible believer; each also reflects a certain ambivalence — a suggestion that fundamentalists themselves may not be thoroughly at peace with the religious authority to which they have subjected themselves.

In order to comprehend why individuals become and remain fundamentalists, it seemed to me imperative to understand how that authority looks to the individual *inside* the discourse. I therefore want to analyze the role, both perceived and actual, that the Bible plays in constituting the authority of fundamentalism. To do so, I will use the tools of that discipline most closely associated with the interpretation of texts — literary theory. At a time when literary critics are experiencing what is almost always called a "crisis" of authority in their own field, the possibilities for a fruitful encounter between fundamentalism and literary study are rich,

1

so rich that I conceive of my present work as a suggestive approach rather than an exhaustive analysis. My own sense of this encounter is informed particularly by the literary theory of Stanley Fish and the methodologies of Michel Foucault. I have found Foucault's notion of *discourse* to be an especially productive means of investigating the authority of Protestant fundamentalism. In Foucault's conception:

> Nothing is fundamental. That is what is interesting in the analysis of society. That is why nothing irritates me so much as these inquiries — which are by definition metaphysical — on the foundations of power in a society or the self-institution of society, etc. These are not fundamental phenomena. There are only reciprocal relations, and the perpetual gaps between intentions in relation to one another. ("Space, Knowledge, and Power" 247)

Accordingly, my study does not seek the ultimate origins of fundamentalism nor does it locate its authority in the specific contributions of powerful individuals. Rather, I attempt to investigate fundamentalist discourse by analyzing the interrelationship of its various aspects. In so doing, I work with a certain irony — the denial of "fundamentals" in the study of a discourse which insists on fundamentals. Yet, ironically, it is this method which allows us not only to perceive fundamentalism as its subjects may perceive it, but to appreciate how its central claim — the sole authority of the Bible — is both true and false, true at the level of personal belief, false at the level of the general discourse. Because the authority of a text is partially constituted by those who interpret that text and because fundamentalism so masterfully effaces the role of interpretation, fundamentalism has been very successful in winning and sustaining its converts. Preachers contend that they do nothing more than expound the plain sense of the Word of God, and so thoroughly do they lard their pronouncements with Bible verses that it is indeed difficult for the ordinary layperson to dispute a preacher's authority, derived as it appears to be from the Word of God itself.

Just as we cannot locate authority exclusively in the text, neither can we locate it exclusively in the persons of individual preachers. As Foucault remarks in *The Discourse on Language,* "We know perfectly well that we are not free to say just anything, that we cannot simply speak of anything, when we like or where we like; not just anyone, finally, may speak of just anything" (216). Even preachers are limited in their authority: they cannot say just anything they want, nor is their considerable power over their flocks an unfettered one. They must adhere to the fundamentalist interpretation of the Bible. The authority of fundamentalism arises in the "reciprocal relations" of text, preachers, commentators, and ordinary readers. And in studying these relations, one confronts the compelling power of the closed system, a power which cannot be localized but is of one cloth, a power woven in and through every thread.

My work has benefited from the contributions of numerous scholars of fundamentalism; I would give special acknowledgement to four of them. Although I will disagree now and again with James Barr, his *Fundamentalism* is indispensable. The astuteness of Barr's observations and the precision of his critique might be measured by the enormous and largely negative attention fundamentalists have since accorded him. Barr's polemical approach to fundamentalism is balanced by the more dispassionate work of Ernest Sandeen, Timothy Weber, and George Marsden, each of whom has shed clear and well-focused light on the historical foundations of modern Protestant fundamentalism.

In choosing a primarily ahistorical approach to this subject (an approach which is not, I trust, anti-historical), I seek to complement not contradict historical studies. It is one thing, and a very necessary thing, to analyze how a discourse itself comes into being, to discover, as Ernest Sandeen did in his pioneering work, the "roots of fundamentalism." But such study has not illuminated, except in the most indirect way, the roots of the fundamental*ist*. Most rank-and-file fundamentalists are dimly aware, at best, of J. N. Darby's dispensationalism, the Princeton Theology, Common Sense philosophy, or even what has come to be known as the Fundamentalist-Modernist Controversy of the 1920s, epitomized by the Scopes Trial. While numerous figures, episodes, and schools of thought have been correctly identified as necessary conditions to the foundation of contemporary fundamentalist discourse, they cannot serve to explain why a given individual makes a personal decision to enter that discourse. One further notes in the discourse itself resolute refusals to acknowledge that historical circumstance or a particular *zeitgeist* plays or ought to play any role whatsoever in influencing doctrine and practice. For example, fundamentalists are pleased to "view themselves as the legitimate heirs of historical New Testament Christianity" (Falwell, ed. 1–2). But this sense of history is better termed a sense of *heritage*. The New Testament church, the theology and polity of which is described in the canonical text, is considered to be canonical itself and thus absolute. Only insofar as Christians throughout the centuries have demonstrated their fidelity to this model do fundamentalists give any credence to eccelesiastical tradition. The writings of the Church Fathers, therefore, are read with caution if they are read at all, the wheat of truth being sifted from the chaff of "Catholicism." The Reformers, however, emerge as heroes struggling to restore the golden age of the New Testament. This perception, dubious as it might be, is nevertheless a decisive component of fundamentalist authority.

On this and similar points, we will ourselves need to cultivate a kind of double vision in order to comprehend doctrinal power — determining how and why particular doctrines are philosophically or historically flawed, while at the same time transcending those flaws in the recognition that fundamentalists themselves would either disagree with or be unaware of negative critique. But whether fundamentalists advance counterarguments or remain oblivious to criticism, their response to outsiders is equally and firmly rooted in their Bible belief. So it is on their use of the biblical text that we must focus, reading that text *with* them in order to read the text *of* fundamentalism.

In consequence of this reading, I have found neither Bible-believing nor Bakker-bashing to be warranted responses to fundamentalism, a conclusion which may well distress enthusiasts of either pursuit. By comprehending how authority is constituted in fundamentalist discourse, one can draw a valid and productive distinction between fundamental*ism* and fundamental*ists,* criticizing the belief while empathizing with the believer. Like that old fundamentalist proverb "love the sinner and hate the sin," it is a difficult but necessary distinction.

This book arises from my doctoral study in the English department at the State University of New York at Buffalo. Then as now, my work has benefited from the erudition and wit of Robert Daly and the support of Neil Schmitz. My collection of primary source material was enhanced by the generosity of Evelyn Confer, Robert Cook, and Craig Schettler. Numerous persons have contributed directly and indirectly to my thinking about fundamentalism, but I owe special thanks to my friends the Rev. Daniel and Julie McCollister, the Rev. Mark Caruana, George Bishop, and the late Michael Horsman. Discussions with my husband, Blair Boone, have been frequent and spirited. They have often ended with his saying, "You owe me a footnote." Doubtless I owe him many, but he is best acknowledged as a perceptive scholar, confidant, and friend.

All biblical quotations are from the King James Version.

Chapter 1

Introduction

All scripture is given by inspiration of God, and is profitable for doctrine, for reproof, for correction, for instruction in righteousness.

2 Tim. 3.16

Even a Baptist pastor, though he may preach without knowing anything else, cannot preach until he knows the Bible.

H. L. Mencken[1]

If asked to explain how Protestant fundamentalists differ from other Christians, a fundamentalist would very likely respond that he or she is a "Bible believer." The fundamentalist might be a member of a Bible church, a regular attendee of Bible studies, a graduate of a Bible college. Whatever the individual's theological persuasion — whether Calvinist or Arminian, for example — he or she would certainly claim that the Bible is the final authority for doctrine and practice. One is reminded of evangelist Billy Graham's frequent use of the clause "the Bible says" — a locution by which he and his doctrine have been commonly identified as fundamentalist or evangelical. Disparaging expressions for fundamentalism — e.g., Bible thumping, the Bible Belt — are an inverse acknowledgement of fundamentalists' distinctive claim to the Bible.

It would seem, in short, that there is a common-sense, generally agreed identification of the Bible with fundamentalism, an identification not normally made with other Christian (and non-Christian) groups for which the Bible is also a sacred text.[2] This curious situation calls for closer examination: why should the Rev. Jerry Falwell, say, be more closely linked to the Bible than the Archbishop of Canterbury? What does the word *Bible,* its iteration, its frequent and perplexing function as an adjective, suggest about fundamentalism?

Only fundamentalists make a point of characterizing themselves as Bible believers. To believe the Bible is to take it literally, to regard every word of it as inerrant and fully divine, to acknowledge no authority above

5

it or equal to it. Protestant fundamentalism, in short, portrays itself as neither more nor less than the authority of God.

It is this last characteristic — this apparent arrogance so typical of fundamentalism — that is at once disturbing and intriguing. Well-worn maxims of American culture — to each his own, everyone is entitled to his own opinion, don't tread on me — our fierce defense of individualism and personal freedoms seems to fall almost completely by the wayside in the fundamentalist world. Even more curiously, fundamentalists espouse Americanist sentiments without awareness of contradiction: those who advocate a strong defense to "keep America free" are often the very same people who send their children to private fundamentalist schools, where library books are scrupulously censored, textbooks without taint of "secular humanism" are used, and the word *evolution* never passes the lips of the biology teacher. "We come at it from an authoritarian point of view," says one fundamentalist pastor, whose Christian school is the subject of sociologist Alan Peshkin's invaluable study *God's Choice* (8).[3]

Little wonder that fundamentalism has often been characterized as an anti-intellectual, reactionary, and authoritarian phenomenon. Richard Hofstadter, in his classic *Anti-intellectualism in American Life*, regards fundamentalism as a significant instance, both formative and derivative, of American anti-intellectualism — the privileging of intuition over reason, single-minded commitment to one idea, hostility towards liberal inquiry. Militant fundamentalists "will tolerate no ambiguities, no equivocations, no reservations, and no criticism"(119). Hofstadter cites numerous fundamentalists deriding books and book-learning, including the renowned evangelist Dwight L. Moody, who put the matter succinctly: "I do not read any book, unless it will help me to understand *the* book" (108).

Church historian Martin Marty has characterized fundamentalism as "a worldwide reaction against many of the mixed offerings of modernity" (*Religion and Republic* 299). He has drawn intriguing parallels between groups which are in fact deeply hostile toward one another. "The echoes of the Iranian militants are loud and clear," Marty wrote in 1980, in reference to Jerry Falwell's use of the term "holy war" ("Fundamentalism Reborn" 38). Fundamentalism appeals to those looking for "authoritarian solutions," Marty believes, and its present resurgence is partially due to contemporary fundamentalists' skillful use of the mass media (*Religion* 300). Yet Marty does not express alarm over this resurgence, believing that fundamentalism "appeals to a rather definite class and personality type." Although fundamentalists have indisputably gained a larger audience for their views, their doctrines are not, Marty says, "the choice of the many" (300–01). In Marty's portrait, fundamentalists seem motivated less by religious belief as such than by psychological disposition, social forces and historical circumstance.

Fundamentalists Anonymous, a self-help group for ex-fundamentalists, regards fundamentalists' use of the Bible as a smoke screen, but unlike Marty, they perceive fundamentalism as a very clear threat, noting that Catholic, Jewish, and Islamic fundamentalists share with their Protestant brethren a common "mindset," one characterized as "authoritarian, intolerant, and compulsive about control." Thus:

> It is not productive to dwell on fundamentalist theology and point out its contradictions and errors. The theology, the idolatry of the Bible as reflected in the doctrine of "literal inerrancy" — these are merely tools, excuses, or alibis for the fundamentalist mindset. Without the mindset, the doctrines wither. ("The Root of the Problem" 3).

These three readings of fundamentalism typify a prevalent attitude toward fundamentalism — that it is, at bottom, an authoritarian phenomenon, one which uses the Bible — or hides behind it — to cloak its agenda in the divine raiment of God's Word. But even if it were true that the Bible furnishes "merely tools, excuses, or alibis" for the fundamentalist's darker purposes, one wonders why these rationales are so often effective, credibility being the acid test of a good excuse. Might not the converse of the Fundamentalists Anonymous position be true: without the doctrines, the mindset withers? Once the Bible has been established as a God-given text, free of error and plain in its message, might it be possible that fundamentalism perpetuates itself in the minds of individual believers, binding them to a certain kind of belief solely because the Bible tells them so?

I have thus far referred to *fundamentalism* as though it were a unified phenomenon, its many adherents believing roughly the same thing, behaving essentially the same way. But as the old joke goes, strand two fundamentalist preachers on a desert island, and within a week each will have started his own church.[4] This question — what is fundamentalism? — must be addressed in some detail.

Among conservative Protestants, one is hard pressed to find a label more loaded and disputed than *fundamentalist*. For some, the label is honorable, for others insulting. Among Christians loosely characterized by outsiders as fundamentalist, there is in fact fierce squabbling over who belongs, who does not, who prefers not to belong, and so on.

One might feel safe in supposing Pat Robertson to be a fundamentalist, but he speaks in tongues. Many self-described fundamentalists believe the charismatic (or Pentecostal) movement is, at best, contrary to the will of God, at worst, a work of the Devil. "On the basis of the Scriptural evidence, we have concluded that tongues have ceased. . . . Consequently we are convinced that the modern tongues movement is not of God" (Sellers 26). Earlier I mentioned Billy Graham in a context which suggested he is a fundamentalist. Again, many would exclude Graham: too "liberal," too ecumenical, he cooperates with mainline Protestants and Roman Catholics — groups which extreme fundamentalists believe are not Christian at all.[5]

Conversely, many conservatives reject the label *fundamentalist*, preferring to call themselves *evangelicals*. As James Barr has observed, *fundamentalism* has negative connotations: it suggests "narrowness, bigotry, obscurantism, and sectarianism" (*Fundamentalism* 2).[6] J. I. Packer, author of the influential defense of biblical inerrancy *"Fundamentalism" and the Word of God,* expresses his own queasiness about the term by putting it in quotation marks. Although he notes that evangelicals are fundamentalist in their doctrine, he also discusses the many reasons *fundamentalism* has become an objectionable term (24-40), concluding that "because of its prejudicial character, and associations, it is not a useful title for Evangelicals today" (169).

Among self-described evangelicals, in short, *fundamentalism* is now reserved as a term for extremism. The journal *Christianity Today* calls itself evangelical; the *Sword of the Lord* tabloid is proudly fundamentalist. Among the readers of *Christianity Today,* an "ethic of civility" prevails, to use James Davison Hunter's useful term. But I must qualify that application by noting that *Christianity Today* itself has expressed alarm over Hunter's discovery of that ethic among evangelical college and seminary students, whose "liberal" views are detailed in the sociologist's study, *Evangelicalism: The Coming Generation.* David Neff, a *Christianity Today* editor, is clearly distressed by some of Hunter's findings, such as the willingness of some students to admit non-Christians to heaven or their reluctance to talk about hell: "we must guard against civility breeding timidity and cancelling the compelling message of salvation through the one and only Way, Truth, and Life" ("The Down Side of Civility" 13). Then again, John R. Rice, late editor of *Sword of the Lord,* attacks *Christianity Today* on exactly this point, averring that moderate evangelicals in general and *Christianity Today* in particular are insufficiently concerned about "soul winning" (the fundamentalist term for proselytizing) (499). Rice further charges that *Christianity Today* "frequently publishes articles by modernists," observing that "although they claim to believe the Bible, they are buddy-buddies with the infidels who spit on the blood of Jesus, deny the inspiration of the Bible and the blood atonement, while they despise us fundamentalists" (147). (Rice is correct insofar as *CT's* editorial taste does not run to the unrelenting and gruesome descriptions of hell favored by the *Sword.*)

The stylistic difference here is clearly spacious, although I am not convinced of any significant disagreements in substance. Neither is James Barr, whose *Fundamentalism* is in fact primarily concerned with those moderates who call themselves evangelicals. While Barr duly notes that many fundamentalists do not like to be called fundamentalists, he argues that there is, in effect, no reason for the scholar not to call a spade a spade: "The fact is that 'fundamentalism' is the normal designation in common English for the phenomenon which we propose to discuss"(3).

Among self-described evangelicals, it is usually a toss-up as to what distresses them most — Barr's critique or his terminology. Carl F. H. Henry, who conducts a sustained attack on Barr in volume 4 of his major opus *God, Revelation and Authority*, quibbles with Barr's use of the term *fundamentalism*, yet he warns the evangelical not to be fooled: "Barr's broad and tireless use of the term *fundamentalism* should not deflect the reader from seeing that Barr objects not simply to an extreme aberration of biblical Christianity, but to historic evangelical orthodoxy as well" (4.100). What then constitutes evangelical doctrine, or as Henry would also have it, "biblical Christianity"? "In brief, the issue becomes the literal sense of an errant Bible, which Barr champions, versus the literal truth of an inerrant Bible, which evangelicals affirm" (4.122).

Indeed, Barr's terminology and the argument which supports it have been used by one fundamentalist source to chide self-described evangelicals. *The Fundamentalist Phenomenon* (edited by Jerry Falwell, written for the most part by two of Falwell's lieutenants, Ed Dobson and Ed Hindson) cites Barr to argue that evangelicalism ought to own up to the fact "that it is not intrinsically different from the mainstream of Fundamentalism!" (6–7).[7] Having given an extensive survey of conservative Protestant groups, Dobson and Hindson conclude, "The one unifying factor in all these movements, without a doubt, is their common adherence to the basic authority of Scripture as the only dependable guide for faith and practice" (53).

Likewise, Alan Peshkin views the biblical inerrancy doctrine as the common trait by which one identifies all *fundamentalists* (25). Robert K. Johnston, who uses the term *evangelical*, notes that all such Christians share

a personal faith in Jesus Christ as Lord and a commitment to the Bible as our sole and binding authority.

Evangelical theologians, thus, distinguish themselves from other theologians within the Christian community by accepting as axiomatic the Bible's inherent authority. (3)

Although Pat Robertson would certainly fit Johnston's definition, there is considerable controversy over whether charismatics might properly be called fundamentalists or evangelicals. *The Fundamentalist Phenomenon* gives a succinct summary of the differences and similarities:

> While Fundamentalists, as a group, violently reject the Pentecostal-Charismatic Movement because of its emphasis on the doctrine of [speaking in] tongues, it must, nevertheless, be recognized that the Pentecostal Movement is based upon an evangelical doctrinal foundation. To that foundation, however, the movement has added a stronger subjective religious experience than is accepted by most conservative Christians. (Falwell, ed. 71)

Thus, while Pentecostals and charismatics give greater emphasis to avenues of divine revelation other than the scriptures — especially in their emphasis on glossolalia — most will agree that the Bible must be the normative text against which all such experiences are measured.[8]

One might wonder at this point, why use the term *fundamentalism* at all? Why not use the terminology favored by one's subjects rather than foisting upon them a label they find offensive? The simple answer is that any choice will end up offending somebody: a fundamentalist like John R. Rice will find the term *evangelical* offensive, because for him it connotes an objectionable liberalism. Barr's justification of the term *fundamentalism* on grounds of common usage is also a sound point. But we must also answer a different question: can one justify the inclusion of what we might call the *Sword*-type Christian and the *Christianity Today*-type Christian in the same category, whatever label one chooses to affix to that category?

There is clearly much common ground shared by the fundamentalist and the evangelical — enough that exclusive attention to one side or the other would result in a distorted view of what is, I am convinced, a single discourse — one which can productively and fairly be called *fundamentalist*.[9] By viewing fundamentalism as a *tendency*, a habit of mind, rather than a discrete movement or phenomenon, we can discern a unified body of discourse, a body of discourse arising from belief in the sole authority of an inerrant Bible. Any given individual can participate, fully or partially, obediently or rebelliously, in this discourse at any given time under any given circumstance. When, for example, I refer to Clark Pinnock as a fundamentalist — an identification cognoscenti will regard as peculiar if not downright offensive — what I mean to identify is Pinnock's *tendency toward fundamentalism* as evidenced by some of what he has to say; I do not mean to characterize him as *a fundamentalist*, thereby pigeonholing him for theological census purposes.

I have pursued this question of terminology in some detail because it is an acute sore point for many of my subjects, and with good enough reason. Fundamentalism is the skeleton in the closet of evangelicalism — the shirttail relation who for compelling reasons cannot nor will not be disowned. We will recognize a compunction toward fundamentalism among evangelicals, a sense of being forced to adopt certain postures and principles they would not otherwise wish to adopt. Conversely, one notices a peculiar anxiety among moderates, a defensiveness about certain positions, a need to justify at ponderous length their espousal of a "non-fundamentalist" position. And it is this force, this tendency toward fundamentalism, that brings us straight back to the question of the Bible.

Without its distinctive method of reading the Bible, Protestant fundamentalism would not exist. I propose to investigate this rather obvious point by examining fundamentalism as a *literary* phenomenon — that is to say in this instance, one in which an authoritative text shapes and motivates discourse. I am attempting to penetrate fundamentalist discourse, attempting to see it as insiders see it, through analyzing how they read the Bible, the consequences of that reading, and the Bible's role, both perceived and actual, in constituting the severe authority of fundamentalism.

To that end, I would first address the widespread misconception that fundamentalists are the village idiots of Christendom — intellectually benighted folk to be pitied or ruthless preachers to be pilloried. Fundamentalist discourse is in fact marked by an unrelenting rationalism, not the irrationalism or emotionalism with which fundamentalism has so often been identified. Anti-intellectual though it may be, Dwight L. Moody's refusal to read books that do not help him "understand *the* book" is neither irrational nor emotionalistic; Moody's religious faith is grounded in his rational comprehension of the biblical text rather than subjective apprehension of the divine. Charles Hodge, a seminal fundamentalist theologian, asserts in his *Systematic Theology* of 1873, "The feelings come from spiritual apprehension of the truth, and not the knowledge of truth from the feelings" (1:178). Hodge's successor, Benjamin B. Warfield, continues in the same vein: "Christianity makes its appeal to right reason, and stands out among all religions, therefore, as distinctively 'the Apologetic religion.' It is solely by reasoning that it has come thus far on its way to kingship" (quoted in Marsden 115). In *The God Who Is There*, Francis Schaeffer, a highly influential twentieth-century theologian, argues throughout this work that orthodox Christianity is a preeminently rational system, open to empirical inquiry. He describes the scriptures as "God's propositional communication to mankind, which not only touch 'religious' truth but also touch the cosmos and history which are open to verification" (108). The 1978 Internationl Conference on Biblical Inerrancy affirmed:

> Those who profess faith in Jesus Christ as Lord and Savior are called
> to show the reality of their discipleship by humbly and faithfully
> obeying God's written Word. To stray from Scripture in faith or
> conduct is disloyalty to our Master.
> Recognition of the total truth and trustworthiness of Holy Scripture
> is essential to a full grasp and adequate confession of its authority.
> (Geisler 493)

While all these statements are explicitly religious — and, some would argue,
therefore subjective — they illustrate the fundamentalist preoccupation
with "truth," and the view that truth is absolute, objective, and found in,
indeed identical with the Bible.

It would be misleading to suggest that fundamentalists recognize no
sources of divine revelation other than the Bible. But all such sources are
ultimately subsumed by the text, their efficacy as revelation therefore
rendered next to nil. Like all Christians, fundamentalists believe that the
incarnation of Christ constituted a divine revelation. They point out,
however, that Christ is reliably known only through scripture. Harold
Lindsell, in *The Battle for the Bible,* demonstrates the priority of the written
word nicely when he says, "It is the Word of God written that reveals the
Word of God incarnate to men. The Bible, then, is *the* Word of God and
it is of this Word we now speak" (30, original emphasis). Although "the
leading of the Holy Spirit" is an integral aspect of fundamentalist theology,
it is stressed that any such subjective encounter with God must be authen-
ticated by scripture. As Richard W. DeHaan of the Radio Bible Class admonishes, "You must test the genuineness of an experience by measuring
it against a reliable, objective standard. And that standard is the Bible,
the Word of God!" (*Charismatic Controversy* 7). Although DeHaan is here
attacking precisely the theology and practice of Pentecostals like television
evangelist Jimmy Swaggart, Swaggart himself asserts that "experiences
must conform to the spirit of God's Word. And if they do not, they should
be rejected out of hand" (8). Because the inner light cannot contradict the
fundamentalist interpretation of scripture — if it does, the subjective
message or feeling is *ipso facto* not of God — a definite priority of the
textual message over personal experience is established.

If fundamentalism is a preeminently *verbal* system, one which takes
a text as its starting point, it is clear that fundamentalism offers textual
critics a fascinating object of investigation. Fundamentalists and literary
scholars alike are devoted to questions of textual interpretation. As Peshkin
discovered, English is considered, after religion, the second most important
subject in the Christian school curriculum: in order to read the Word of
God competently, one must be literate (56). Going their secular counterparts

one better, fundamentalists are bound to view correct interpretation as a matter of eternal life or death. If one's eternal destiny depends on a right relationship with God, and if that God is reliably known only through the Bible, it follows that one must read, and read correctly. Put another way, there is no comparison between the risk of publishing a dimwitted scholarly article and the danger of burning in hell. To move beyond reading the text *of* fundamentalism to reading the text *with* fundamentalism is a sobering experience, one I hope to convey throughout this work.

At the risk of overgeneralizing, I would now give a brief overview of how fundamentalists regard and read the Bible. The fundamentalist believes the Bible is wholly without error, whether doctrinal, historical, scientific, grammatical or clerical. If the text is not inerrant, fundamentalists believe, it cannot be trusted — and if the text is untrustworthy, one has no grounds for believing *anything* it says. There is in fundamentalism a strong sense that the Bible is to be "taken literally," that it "means what it says." Many fundamentalists are *dispensationalists*, using a distinctive method of textual division and classification whereby seven dispensations, or ages, are distinguished in the biblical material. One of the virtues of dispensationalism is its support of the inerrancy doctrine: apparent intratextual contradictions are often resolved by identifying dispensational differences.

Whatever their theological or stylistic differences, all fundamentalists agree that the Bible stands alone as the final word on all matters, sacred and secular. Everyone, clergy and laity alike, is to read the Bible often and to study it thoroughly. Fundamentalists believe the Bible to be perspicuous, its meaning deducible by the common reader. "In ninety-nine out of a hundred cases, the meaning that the plain man gets out of the Bible is the correct one" (Reuben A. Torrey, quoted in Marsden 61). The Bible becomes something of an icon and sacramental object. Frequent use of the word *Bible* as a modifier (Bible school, Bible church, Bible belief) signifies the high status of the text. The pulpit is usually placed in the center of the sanctuary, signifying the centrality of the preaching of the Word; this practice stands in marked symbolic contrast to the central position of the altar in churches which view the eucharistic celebration as the focal point of worship. The fundamentalist altar, upon which lies an open Bible, will be placed behind or before the pulpit. Sermons are expository: the preacher bases his address on a biblical text, and the more adept he is at cross-referencing his primary text with other scriptural passages the better his sermon is considered to be. The *New Scofield Reference Bible*, popular among fundamentalist clergy and laity alike, includes a chain-reference system, enabling the reader to trace key "doctrines," e.g., "inspiration," throughout the scriptures: the references are termed by the editors "among the most important and useful features" of this text (xiv).

It is already apparent that preachers, teachers, and commentators play a significant role in this religion of the open book, this book accessible to the "plain man." We will see how textual interpreters contribute to the discourse and how that contribution is itself authoritative, influencing the "plain man," the ordinary reader who prays for the Holy Spirit's guidance in understanding the Word of God. In my analysis of fundamentalist discourse I am supposing, with Michel Foucault,

> that in every society the production of discourse is at once controlled, selected, organised and redistributed according to a certain number of procedures, whose role is to avert its powers and its dangers, to cope with chance events, to evade its ponderous, awesome materiality. (*Discourse* 216)

In identifying and describing the production of fundamentalist discourse, this study attempts to discover what Foucault calls the "rules" of discourse, rules which operate "according to a sort of uniform anonymity, on all individuals who undertake to speak in this discursive field" (*Archaeology* 63). These rules, often enough implicit or hidden, govern what may be said and who enjoys the right to say it.

Because the rules of discourse are impersonal, the question of which comes first — the discourse or the discoursers — does not arise. Causation is not denied, but it is envisioned as a circular rather than a linear process, and even circular fails as a thoroughly adequate conception. The "web," to use Foucault's useful term, of text, commentary, personal experience, upbringing, and personality cannot be apprehended by attempting to determine which of these factors comes "first." Rather, we come nearer to comprehending the fundamentalist phenomenon by observing how its various aspects play with and against one another in perpetual process.

Because fundamentalism has recently been the focus of renewed public attention, due to the various actions and antics of prominent televangelists, it is especially important to recognize that the power of a discourse does not arise entirely from the conscious practices of individuals in positions of leadership. Even prior to the Bakker and Swaggart scandals, secular critics traditionally viewed television evangelists with a cynical eye, supposing that a Jerry Falwell or an Oral Roberts sits alone late at night, pondering how best to loosen the pursestrings of the faithful and how best to induce the legion of faithless to enter the fold and fork over their cash too. Although one would not deny that strategic thinking occurs, an evangelist's empire is not entirely under his own control, as recent events have so clearly demonstrated. The role of the subject, whether leader or follower, is transcribed by the larger discourse in which he participates. No single individual is smart enough or powerful enough to manipulate fundamentalist discourse fully, and in certain ways, the discourse manipulates him. To enjoy credibility, one must ensure that one's own discourse is following the explicit and implicit rules of the general discourse. No single individual can master a discourse, and thus no single individual can achieve mastery *over* a discourse. As Foucault has observed, discourse is characterized by:

> Different *oeuvres*, dispersed books, that whole mass of texts that belong to a single discursive formation — and so many authors who know or do not know one another, criticize one another, invalidate one another, pillage one another, meet without knowing it and obstinately intersect their unique discourses in a web of which they are not the masters, of which they cannot see the whole, and of whose breadth they have a very inadequate idea. (*Archaeology* 126)

The personal power of the preacher pales in comparison with the impersonal power of fundamentalist discourse. The preacher's authority exists in direct proportion to his appropriation of the authority of the biblical text, a text which he expounds in accordance with the particular rules of fundamentalist discourse. And because that text is to be found in every strand of the "web," it is with the Bible that analysis must begin.

Chapter 2

By Inspiration of God: The Plain Book

The Bible is a plain book. It is intelligible by the people. And they have the right and are bound to read and interpret it for themselves; so that their faith may rest on the testimony of the Scriptures, and not that of the Church.

Charles Hodge[1]

Shakespeare is an inexhaustible source of occult readings . . . yet at the same time he is believed to speak plainly, about most of human life, to any literate layman. Like the scriptures, he is open to all, but at the same time so dark that special training, organized by an institution of considerable size, is required for his interpretation.

Frank Kermode[2]

If the Bible is the sole authority for fundamentalists, it must be accessible to every reader. If there is to be no institutional authority in interpretation, it follows that no such authority can be considered necessary. Although Shakespeare too is widely believed to be "open to all," literary critic Frank Kermode also alludes to the equally wide consensus that not just anyone can interpret *well*. The fact is, most literary critics would not dream of setting an untutored person loose on *Hamlet*, much less granting unqualified acceptance of what such a person might discover in *Hamlet*. But Charles Hodge seems confident that the Bible can indeed be read without benefit of commentary or an *a priori* doctrinal scheme into which one can place one's reading. Popular fundamentalist literature is rife with accounts of the unchurched, biblically uneducated reader happening upon a Bible, and by reading therein, coming to what is usually called "a saving knowledge of the Lord Jesus Christ."[3] Although conversion on this basis may seem improbable (what if the reader haplessly turns to Leviticus or Ecclesiastes?), it is a commonplace of fundamentalism that any reader, unaided by clergy or even long-suppressed Sunday School training, can read successfully by him or her self. The biblical text,

17

moreover, contains the message of salvation, acceptance of which leads
to eternal bliss, rejection of which ensures damnation, defined not as mere
annihilation but as "that state of conscious suffering which continues
eternally" (*New Scofield Reference Bible*, note to John 3.16). Unlike squab-
bles over valid readings of *Hamlet*, a correct reading of the Bible is for
the fundamentalist a matter of utmost gravity.

Hodge explicitly contrasts the authority of the individual reading with
that of institutional authority, a polemical habit of long standing in Protestantism to be sure but one which is carried to its logical end in Protestant
fundamentalism. Kermode has noted that, in contrast to the Roman Catholic
tradition, "extreme Protestant theology believed that the text, accepted
by a grace-illumined mind, was in itself enough. . . . It is the presence or
absence of a *church*, and the hierarchical rigor of that church, that makes
the difference" ("Can We Say Absolutely Anything We Like?" 163).

Indeed, mainline Protestant critiques of fundamentalism attack fundamentalism at precisely this point, appealing overtly or covertly to Protestant
church tradition. Gabriel Fackre finds fundamentalism wanting by measuring it against what he calls "classical Christianity," saying, "The Scriptures
constitute the source, the church the resource, and the world the setting
for theological assertions" (34). Similarly, Eric Gritsch, a Lutheran, is
particularly bothered by fundamentalists' failure to practice infant baptism,
a sacrament he views as "commanded" in scripture, without, however,
making it explicit that the Lutheran doctrine of *infant* baptism is itself an
interpretation of scripture, and therefore part of church tradition (92-94).

Because fundamentalists do not bow the knee to pope or prelate,
because they do not appear to grant any institution rights over the individual reader in matters of interpretation, they necessarily must place
immense weight on the text itself to instruct its readers aright. In the next
two chapters, I want to explore how fundamentalists conceive of their text.
At the risk of getting ahead of my argument, I would note that one cannot
adequately appreciate the power of textual *interpreters* — my primary
concern — until one has a basic understanding of how the text itself is
perceived and why that perception is problematic.[4] The notion that
extreme Protestants do *not* possess a "church" to govern interpretation
arises from the rhetorical and structural skill with which fundamentalism
denies institutional authority, all the while possessing a *de facto* institutional
structure which is all the more powerful for being hidden.

Readers familiar with current literary theory will no doubt have
noticed by now intriguing similarities between the issues raised by fundamentalist textual interpretation and those being vigorously debated among
literary critics. Because there is at present little consensus among literary
critics regarding the proper interpretation of texts, the manner in which

one discovers their meaning, and which texts we should be reading anyhow, canon-formation having become the locus of hot dispute, we are witnessing the distressing spectacle of the hamfisted and the hamstrung. Competing theorists slug it out in the journals, in some cases genuinely unable to communicate because the philosophical grounds on which their arguments are based are radically opposed, while others lapse into epistemological despair, leaping to the morbid conclusion that because no one is right, everyone is right — a state of paralysis hardly conducive to the confident production of meaningful work.

Without vastly oversimplifying, one can say that this crisis of authority in literary criticism is the collective nightmare of fundamentalism. It is for this reason that fundamentalists insist authority must be grounded exclusively in the text; in Harold Lindsell's words, words which will resonate uncannily for literary critics, "I am contending that once biblical inerrancy is scrapped, it leads inevitably to the denial of biblical truths that are inextricably connected with matters of faith and practice" (139). Compare Lindsell's statement with the contention of literary theorist E. D. Hirsch that "without the stable determinacy of meaning there can be no knowledge in interpretation, nor any knowledge in the many humanistic disciplines based upon textual interpretation" (*Aims* 1).

It remains to be seen, of course, whether the stability and certainty offered by either Lindsell or Hirsch stand up in theory and practice. In analyzing fundamentalist textual interpretation, I will be describing fundamentalist concerns with particular reference to the work of E. D. Hirsch and analyzing their interpretative practices with reference to Stanley Fish, an opponent of Hirsch who locates authority not in the "determinate meaning" of the text but in the collective determinations of the "interpretive community." I will focus on the fundamentalist doctrine of *biblical inerrancy* — its establishment, consequences for exegesis, and perceived necessity for authority. That most well-known and at times misunderstood fundamentalist practice of "taking the Bible literally" will be analyzed as a tendency following from the postulation of inerrancy, a means whereby fundamentalists attempt to ward off perversities of interpretation, and most importantly, a key factor in deploying the power of fundamentalism through the doctrine of literal hellfire.

By way of introducing my analysis of fundamentalist textual interpretation, I want to summarize the theories of Hirsch and Fish, and address how I will apply them to the subject at hand. Interpretive anarchy threatens, E. D. Hirsch warns, unless one upholds the "determinacy" of meaning. Being determinate, meaning must be fixed, unchanging, and determined *by* someone. For Hirsch, that someone can be none other than the author of the text in question: for an interpretation to have "validity," the interpreter "must be willing to measure his interpretation against a genuinely discriminating norm, and the only compelling normative principle that has ever been brought forward is the old-fashioned ideal of rightly understanding what the author meant" (*Validity* 26). His theory requires that a scrupulous distinction be maintained between the *meaning* of a text and its *significance:*

> *Meaning* is that which is represented by a text; it is what the author meant by his use of a particular sign sequence; it is what the signs represent. *Significance,* on the other hand, names a relationship between that meaning and a person, or a conception, or a situation, or indeed anything imaginable. (*Validity* 8)

"Failure to consider this simple and essential distinction," Hirsch continues, "has been the source of enormous confusion in hermeneutic theory." As a champion of determinate meaning, Hirsch has devoted much of his career to decrying subjectivism and relativism in textual interpretation.

In contrast to Hirsch, Stanley Fish argues that authority in interpretation arises from not from the "valid" interpretation of texts but from its situation within "interpretive communities." By focusing on the role interpreters inevitably play in determining the meaning of a text, Fish has argued persuasively that the text does not, indeed cannot, possess or generate meaning in and of itself. Although Fish rejects Hirsch's defense of determinate meaning, he does not believe that the door is then opened for any and all interpretations. The traditional opposition between "objectivity" and "subjectivity" in interpretation becomes, for Fish, a false dichotomy:

> An interpretive community is not objective because as a bundle of interests, of particular purposes and goals, its perspective is interested rather than neutral; but by the very same reasoning, the meanings and texts produced by an interpretive community are not subjective because they do not proceed from an isolated individual but from a public and conventional point of view. (14)

By insisting on the sole authority of the biblical text, fundamentalists are bound to defend the determinacy of meaning. Like Hirsch, they argue that textual *meaning* has been determined, once for all, by the will of its author — in this case, God. The scriptures are therefore to be interpreted prayerfully, the reader asking the author for enlightenment. Textual *significance,* on the other hand, will come into play when the reader applies scriptural teaching to practical concerns in his or her own life or to worldly affairs. The individual suffering from illness may find a particular psalm of immense personal comfort. The woman contemplating marriage to an "unsaved" man will find significance in 2 Cor. 6. 14: "Be ye not unequally yoked together with unbelievers." Ronald Reagan, seeking biblical authority for defense appropriations, cited Luke 14.31: "Or what king, going to make war against another king, sitteth not down first, and consulteth whether he be able with ten thousand to meet him that cometh against him with twenty thousand?"[5]

There is little difference, in short, between Hirsch's interpretive theory and that espoused by fundamentalists, although fundamentalist interpreters do not generally use Hirsch's exact terminology. The logical and practical problems inherent in Hirsch's theory are similar to those inherent in fundamentalist interpretive theory. Stanley Fish's critiques of Hirschian interpretation and his definition of the interpretive community are therefore useful in comprehending fundamentalism. Applied to fundamentalism, Fish's notion of interpretive community would look something like this. Because fundamentalists share certain presuppositions and doctrines, they interpret the biblical text in a distinctive and relatively uniform way. Because Roman Catholics, say, behave similarly as members of an interpretive community, they too will arrive at interpretive conclusions reflecting the specific interests of their community. Disagreements *between* communities are, therefore, hardly surprising: "The assumption in each community will be that the other is not correctly perceiving the 'true text,' but the truth will be that each perceives the text (or texts) its interpretive strategies demand and call into being" (Fish 171). Disagreements *within* communities are thus potentially resolvable by appeal to the set of presuppositions or interpretive strategies upon which that community is based. A fundamentalist might attack a colleague's interpretation on grounds that it undermines biblical inerrancy; a Catholic interpreter might charge that a colleague shows insufficient regard for a relevant papal encyclical.

Fish offers little hope, however, for determining the truth or falsity of competing claims advanced by different interpretive communities. Fish would argue, moreover, that it is often the case that members of such communities cannot even talk to each other: "unless someone is willing to entertain the possibility that his beliefs are wrong, he will be unable even to hear an argument that constitutes a challenge to them" (299). Although the interpretive community maintains authority in microcosm, the possibility of a unified, macrocosmic authority is effectively denied. Fish's theory thus affords us little basis for judging authoritative claims from a position outside the community. The best we can do is to *observe* communities at work, determining the internal bases for their assertions. Eventually, I will take up this problem again — for I do think it imperative that one be able to *question* the authority of communities. First, it will be necessary to view our community at work defining its doctrines of the Bible and interpreting the Bible accordingly.

Chapter 3

For Doctrine:
The Inerrant Text

*No one, as far as I know, holds that the English translation
of the Bible is absolutely infallible and inerrant.*

Reuben A. Torrey, 1907[1]

*Why not investigate Trinity Baptist College where the King
James Version is the Word of God in every classroom as
well as in the pulpit?*

Trinity Baptist College, 1981[2]

If the Bible is not free from all error, fundamentalists would no longer
have sure grounds for their faith. They would flounder, they themselves
claim, in a sea of subjective uncertainty. "Christianity is founded upon the
Bible," says J. Gresham Machen, the last of the Princeton theologians.
"[Christian] Liberalism on the other hand is founded upon the shifting
emotions of sinful men" (79). Contemporary evangelical college students
in Hunter's *The Coming Generation* agree. One student remarks: "If the
Bible isn't true, everything in my life would be so tentative. I think there
would be no rock to go back to. Why hold so tightly to my faith if it is
not even stable?" (30). Another says, "If we can't believe the Bible is our
authority, then we really don't have much besides an emotional experience
or some kind of abstract feeling" (30). Hunter himself credits the logic of
biblical inerrancy: "When it is allowed, as it is increasingly so in
Evangelicalism, to interpret the Bible subjectivistically and to see portions
of the Scripture as symbolic or nonbinding, the Scriptures are divested
of their authority to compel obedience" (184).

If the Bible is to function as the sole authority in fundamentalism,
however, several troublesome questions immediately arise. Suppose God's
text has, through human agency, become untrustworthy or corrupt.
Suppose important aspects of the creation narrative are inevitably "lost
in translation" from ancient Hebrew to English. Suppose the Bible is not
a coherent, divinely inspired book at all, but a collection of diverse,
humanly written texts which are a mosaic witness to Judaeo-Christian

religious belief. If any of these suppositions is in fact the case, it is obvious that I can no longer open the King James Version here on my desk and read with total confidence, knowing that each and every word is the very word of God.

For fundamentalists, the truth and authority of scripture are inextricably connected with biblical inerrancy, the primary doctrine whereby fundamentalists attempt to counter these threatening propositions. If the Bible is one's only reliable source of divine revelation and if it turns out to be riddled with errors, fundamentalism would be fatally undercut. Although Harold Lindsell asserts, "I do not know anyone who believes in inerrancy who says that if one error were found in Scripture, he would then give up the Christian faith in its entirety" (162), *The Battle for the Bible*, in its entirety, belies that claim, with Lindsell arguing that "every deviation away from inerrancy ends up by casting a vote in favor of limited inerrancy. Once limited inerrancy is accepted, it places the Bible in the same category with every other book that has ever been written" (203). It is generally maintained, explicit and implicitly, that one proven "error" in the Bible invalidates the entire text, and by implication Christian faith.

In *The Southern Baptist Holy War*, Joe Edward Barnhart describes the anxiety of Southern Baptists; the denomination's current upheaval over the inerrancy question "faces head-on the issue of ultimate authority. If Christians are left to sift through the Bible to separate the credible from the incredible, will the Bible no longer be the Christian's final court of appeal? Will there be any final court of appeal?" (35).

If the Bible is wrong in its cosmogony, for example, then how can we know it is right about the resurrection of Christ, without which, Paul says, "is our preaching vain, and your faith is also vain" (1. Cor. 15.14b)? Indeed, how can we know Paul is right in deeming one's faith "vain"? Maybe he was mistaken, or miscopied, or mistranslated, and it does not matter whether Christ was raised from the dead, and maybe nothing matters at all — so it appears to fundamentalists, imagining themselves either steadfast in absolute truth or whirling in the vortex of nihilism. Thus Francis Schaeffer, arguing for the historicity of Adam and Eve, says:

> If Paul is wrong in this factual statement about Eve's coming from Adam [1 Cor. 11.8], there is no reason to have certainty in the authority of any New Testament factual statement, including the factual statement that Christ rose physically from the dead. (*No Final Conflict* 33-34)

Gleason L. Archer observes that while the story of Jesus and his resurrection is quite fantastic to the natural mind, it must be believed for

salvation (58). Although the literality of the resurrection, i.e., a bodily resurrection, is disbelieved by some Christians, Archer is nevertheless in plentiful
company stating that some sort of "faith in Christ" is necessary to salvation. But he immediately infers:

> We must therefore conclude that *any* event or fact related in Scripture
> — whether it pertains to doctrine, science, or history — is to be
> accepted by the Christian as totally reliable and trustworthy, no
> matter what modern scientists or philosophers may think of it. (59,
> original emphasis)

The logic of biblical inerrancy is palpable. If God is omniscient, and
if he is the author of the scriptural text, it follows that the text cannot
contain mistakes, whether in content or form. If it should be found to
contain errors, through some indiscernible will of its author, it remains
problematic that an omniscient, omnipotent, and perfectly good being
should be content to allow errors to have come into existence in his
written work. As I have just made apparent, there is a family resemblance
between biblical inerrancy and the problem of evil; both the inerrantist
and the theodicist are faced with the dual difficulty of making intellectual
sense of the problem, and defending the character and competence of the
God in which each believes.

In order to appreciate the distinctiveness of the fundamentalist position,
it is helpful to consider briefly how other Protestants read the Bible even
as they too consider it a sacred text open to all readers. While inspiration
is a difficult notion, and therefore generative of many nuances, it is fair
to say that many Protestants believe the biblical text *contains* the word
of God, or that particular passages *become* the word of God as they speak
to the reader in his careful and prayerful encounter with the text. Properly
speaking, the Bible is not the Word of God at all; Christ is the Word, the
logos, and the Bible is important insofar as it reveals the Word incarnate.
As Eric Gritsch argues, against fundamentalism:

> Those who are aware of the difference between God (who cannot
> be reached through any human enterprise) and mortal human
> existence in space and time, will not have ultimate trust in the Bible
> as a book. They will agree with the best ecumenical insight that God's
> revelation in Christ is self-authenticating. (59)

For Paul Tillich, the Bible is less revelation itself than a record of revelation; revelation occurs in a profoundly dialectical encounter between God
and man, the biblical text being the report of such engagements:

The Bible is a document both of the divine self-manifestation and of the way in which human beings have received it. . . . The basic error of fundamentalism is that it overlooks the contribution of the receptive side in the revelatory situation and consequently identifies *one* individual and conditioned form of receiving the divine with the divine itself. (4)

In *Scripture, Tradition, and Infallibility,* Dewey Beegle articulates a much more conservative view of biblical revelation, but one which still finds him at odds with the fundamentalist. "In all essential matters of faith and practice . . . Scripture is authentic, accurate, and trustworthy," Beegle claims, in proper fundamentalist parlance. But he continues, "It is the indispensable record of revelation, product of inspiration, and source of authority" (308). It is exactly by placing the words *revelation, inspiration,* and *authority* in prepositional phrases that he provokes fundamentalist ire — for the fundamentalist will contend that the Bible *is* revelation, inspiration, and authority. Because Beegle acknowledges the essential humanity of the text — God spoke through human writers, and the agency of the latter cannot be discounted — he is untroubled by such phenomena as grammatical errors or disagreements between biblical writers narrating the same event.

But these textual phenomena will pose grave difficulties for proponents of biblical inerrancy. *Inerrancy* is, after all, a non-relative term. Like *unique* or *black*, it ought not to admit of modification. Limited or "virtual" inerrancy is as nonsensical as constructions like "more unique" or "blacker than," as careful writers generally agree. Thus when we speak of biblical inerrancy, we should mean that the Bible is without any kind of error, however paltry or inconsequential. This would seem to be the determination of the 1978 International Conference on Biblical Inerrancy, whose "some 300" attendees drafted "The Chicago Statement on Biblical Inerrancy" (Geisler ix):

Being wholly and verbally God-given, Scripture is without error or fault in all its teaching, no less in what it states about God's acts in creation, about the events of world history, and about its own literary origins under God, than in its witness to God's saving grace in individual lives.

The authority of Scripture is inescapably impaired if this total divine inerrancy is in any way limited or disregarded, or made relative to a view of truth contrary to the Bible's own; and such lapses bring serious loss to both the individual and the Church. (Geisler 494)

This passage (points 4 and 5 of the document's "short statement") reflects several important tenets of the inerrancy doctrine: 1) the *entire* text is divinely authored, down to the very words — choice and syntax; 2) the text is a reliable source of secular, e.g., scientific and historical, knowledge, as well as spiritual or religious truth; 3) what the text says about itself must be taken as the starting point of interpretation; and 4) the text cannot be authoritative as a whole unless it be free of error in the smallest part.

But one is left with numerous difficulties, foremost among them being the identity of the "text." Are any or all translations, for example, the word of God? If so, verbal inspiration would seem a mind-boggler, unless we extend the reach of divine inspiration to include translators (which fundamentalists do not). So if translations are not divinely inspired, it would seem that inerrancy has practical value for none but those interpreters thoroughly fluent in ancient Hebrew and New Testament Greek. On what grounds is one asked to take at face value the text's testimony to itself? Does this not amount to begging the question — requiring *a priori* assent to fundamentalist religion, which itself asserts that one is converted by, not before, the text? The precise meaning of *error* must be defined. Either the creation narrative is erroneous because it says God created the earth in six days, or interpreters have erred in taking the word *day* literally. But if the error is on our part as interpreters, are we not allowing science to judge scripture, a practice Archer, for one, explicitly forbids?

For most readers, such questions about texts do not ordinarily arise. If there are inaccuracies in Melville's accounts of whaling or in his taxonomy of whales, we do not then claim that *Moby Dick* is an errant work, one which cannot be valued for its larger themes concerning man and nature. The question, "Is *Moby Dick* true?" is, in this sense of *truth*, nonsensical. In Wittgensteinian terms, the question cannot be asked while playing the language game of literature. We are quite familiar, however, with the essential impossiblity of translation. We know that no translator's *Divine Comedy* can "be" Dante's *Commedia*. John Ciardi, one translator of Dante, describes the impossibility of exact translation well by using a musical analogy:

> I believe that the process of rendering from language to language is better conceived as a "transposition" than as a "translation," for "translation" implies a series of word-for-word equivalents that do not exist across language boundaries any more than piano sounds exist in the violin. (9)

As for the text's testimony to itself, we have become quite familiar in the modern period with unreliable narrators. I think especially of such works as Faulkner's *Absalom, Absalom* and Nabokov's *Pale Fire* when I say that many texts not only provoke us but invite us to question the narrators' personae, their veracity, and their intentions. Even when the narrator is not a shifty character, we take care to establish the narrator's point of view and to distinguish the voice of the narrator from that of the author. In all walks of life, textual and non-textual, we verify self-testimony by using external evidence appropriate to the case. We ask if a defendant's testimony squares with the evidence — whether empirical evidence or the testimony of other witnesses to the alleged crime — and we do not hesitate to convict him on that basis, even as he loudly proclaims his innocence while being escorted from the courtroom. Many of us would not automatically believe a neighbor who claims that, while washing dishes one morning, he was visited by the Mother of God. Like the Jews denounced by Paul, we would require a sign. Or, like the fundamentalist, we might denounce the very idea of the Mother of God as papist poppycock.

The essential unverifiability of religious experience accounts for some of these disparities between the readers of sacred and secular texts. There is finally no way to verify someone's vision of the Virgin Mary; neither can one empirically verify the divine inspiration of a text. From a literary-theoretical standpoint, we can neither affirm nor deny the existence of a God-written text. This does not mean, however, that literary theory becomes ineffectual in analyzing fundamentalist interpretation. If the text is inspired, it is nonetheless read and interpreted by humans, whose fallibility is uncontested. One might respond that those humans are inspired by the Holy Spirit to interpret God's Word rightly, but it is interesting to note that fundamentalists themselves are generally reluctant to pursue this notion to its logical extreme. Fundamentalists stress the "objectivity" of their text, deploring subjectivism as an epistemological and theological threat. They would join E. D. Hirsch in attacking the "radical historicism" of those interpreters in any discipline who believe that the meaning of a text is in any way determined by the historical context of the interpreter; indeed, Hirsch identifies Bultmann as a prime offender in the field of biblical exegesis (*Validity* viii). Perhaps it is not surprising therefore that Hirsch's doctrine of determinate meaning and his defense of objectivity in interpretation have been recognized and enthusiastically applauded by fundamentalist interpreters. Carl F. H. Henry, for example, commends Hirsch for his emphasis on objectivity and authorial consciousness (4.312-15). Henry's own definition of the biblical interpreter's task is grounded squarely in Hirsch's theory:

We must insist that ideally the interpreter shares the objective meaning of the inspired biblical writers as expressed in conceptual-verbal form; we must repudiate recent notions of the historicity of understanding as destructive not only of the normativity of any and all communication but as self-destructive.

At stake in these alternatives is nothing less than either forfeiting or preserving the truth and Word of the God of biblical revelation. (4.315)

As fundamentalist interpreters attempt to determine the objective meaning of their inerrant text, they cannot fail to address the numerous questions raised by their doctrines of the text. Having given an introductory sense of these issues, I now want to look more closely at how fundamentalists themselves address them. Primary sources are copious. I take as representative works the writings of the Princeton theologians, whose work in the late nineteenth and early twentieth centuries, *contra* the "higher criticism," effectively established the contemporary doctrine of inerrancy; J.I. Packer's *"Fundamentalism" and the Word of God* (published in 1958; still widely read and cited); Lindsell's *Battle for the Bible* (1976); and the above-mentioned "Chicago Statement" (1978), representing as it does the closest we might come to present consensus on the question.[3]

We have seen that fundamentalists defend inerrancy as necessary to faith itself. Indeed, the creeds of fundamentalist organizations almost invariably begin with a statement confessing faith in an inerrant Bible; confession of belief in God follows.[4] But we would be greatly mistaken in believing that inerrancy is the simple concept it first appears. I began the chapter by citing Reuben A. Torrey, who declares candidly that translations are not inerrant. Yet Torrey is an inerrantist, and the full context of that quotation provides a useful encapsulation of how fundamentalists, past and present, conceive of biblical inerrancy:

No one, as far as I know, holds that the English translation of the Bible is absolutely infallible and inerrant. The doctrine held by many is that the Scriptures *as originally given* were absolutely infallible and inerrant, and that our English translation is a *substantially accurate* rendering of the Scriptures as originally given. We do not possess the original manuscripts of the Bible. These original manuscripts were copied many times with great care and exactness, but naturally some errors crept into the copies that were made. We now possess so many good copies that by comparing one with another, we can tell with great precision just what the original text was. Indeed, for all practical purposes the original text is now settled. There is not one important doctrine that hangs upon any doubtful reading of the text. (17)

Torrey's exposition of the inerrancy doctrine is unsettling. Although we had assumed a need for fluency in the biblical languages, according to Torrey, even that will not help; the only inerrant texts are the autographs, which are, regrettably, lost. But we need not be alarmed: enough secondary texts exist that we can, in effect, establish the autographs. "The original text is now settled." Torrey establishes the original text by traversing a slippery slope, a slope littered with such phrases as "substantially accurate," "great precision," and "for all practical purposes." There is nothing wrong with these phrases in themselves. We would readily use them to describe, say, the Riverside Shakespeare, but then again, neither we nor the Riverside editors are claiming that these texts of Shakespeare are "inerrant." Lindsell echoes Torrey, but makes the claim unmistakably explicit: "Anyone who has doubts about the accuracy of the Scriptures that have come down to us by transmission through copyists is misinformed. We can say honestly that the Bible we have today is the Word of God" (37)

Torrey's statement is also noteworthy for its emphasis on "important doctrine." Torrey seems willing to ignore the trivial matters which now preoccupy his successors; Christian faith does not stand or fall with determining who was high priest when David ate the temple shewbread.[5] Princeton theologian Charles Hodge was likewise untroubled by minor textual discrepancies, expressing his relative nonchalance in this famous analogy: "No sane man would deny that the Parthenon was built of marble, even if here and there a speck of sandstone should be detected in its structure" (170). The "Chicago Statement" elaborates on these specks in its Article XIII:

> We. . . deny that inerrancy is negated by Biblical phenomena such as a lack of modern technical precision, irregularities of grammar or spelling, observational descriptions of nature, the reporting of falsehoods, the use of hyperbole and round numbers, the topical arrangement of material, variant selections of material in parallel accounts, or the use of free citations. (Geisler 496)

One may well respond, what is the point in using the term *inerrancy* at all? In order to address that question, it is helpful to investigate the major sub-points of the inerrancy doctrine. 1) Inspiration is *plenary*, or verbal. That is, not only the ideas or "message" but the very words of scripture are inspired. Inerrantists protest with great vigor, however, that verbal inspiration is not equivalent to dictation. 2) Christ himself is said to teach the inerrancy of scripture; his authority and perfect knowledge are undermined if one disbelieves that teaching. 3) Inerrancy is properly attributed only to the (lost) autographs; copies and translations are not necessarily inerrant.

Hodge defends verbal inspiration succinctly: "The thoughts are the words. The two are inseparable" (164). Machen agrees: "language is valuable only as the expression of thought. The English word 'God' has no particular virtue in itself. . . . Its importance depends altogether upon the meaning which is attached to it" (110). So if God has inspired every word of the text, if he is the author of the text, then logic would seem to require that he dictated the text to the various human writers of the Bible. Indeed the human writers are not writers at all but stenographers. According to Princeton theologian B.B. Warfield, the scriptures are "not as man's report to us of what God says, but as the very Word of God itself, spoken by God himself through human lips and pens" ("The Inspiration of the Bible" 71). Yet although this operation sounds like dictation, Warfield insists that it is not, calling those who so construe it "dishonest, careless, ignorant or over-eager controverters" of the fundamentalist position ("Inspiration and Criticism" 397). Rather, says Warfield, each word of the text "was at one and the same time the consciously self-chosen word of the writer and the divinely-inspired word of the Spirit" (399). Clearly, such an operation would be miraculous but just as clearly fundamentalists seem anxious to preserve active human agency in the writing of the biblical texts.[6] Nevertheless, one perceives an interesting parallel here between the fundamentalist doctrine of the Bible and the Islamic doctrine of the Koran, despite explicit denials of any parallel. J. I. Packer, for example, claims that fundamentalists do not have a "superstitious regard for the original Hebrew and Greek words (like that of Islam for its Koran, which is held to consist essentially of Arabic words, and therefore to be untranslatable). . ." (89-90). The literary theorist Edward Said has contrasted Christianity and Islam by observing that in Christianity the Word enters history, creating thereby a necessary acknowledgement of the human dimension of scripture. Yet fundamentalism seems more akin to Islam as Said describes it: "Since the Koran is the result of a unique event, the literal 'descent' into worldiness of a text, as well as its language and form, are then to be viewed as stable and complete" (*The World, the Text, and the Critic* 37).

Where Moslems benefit from consistency on this point, fundamentalists experience two major difficulties in attempting to reconcile verbal inspiration with human co-authorship of the Bible and translatability. One is the matter of dictation; their protestations to the contrary, dictation seems a necessary concomitant of verbal inspiration. The inherent insufficiency of translations is an obvious corollary, one which goes a long way toward explaining why the King James Version is the only translation acknowledged by certain fundamentalists, and why there is constant anxiety among all fundamentalists as to the "soundness" of other translations. Some fundamentalist preachers organized book-burnings of the Revised Standard Verison, a.k.a. "The Bible of Antichrist," published in complete form in 1952; ironically, the New International Version (completed in 1978), the contemporary translation currently favored by fundamentalists, is very similar to the RSV (Noll 110-11).

Warfield's main contribution to the inerrancy discussion, however, is his attempt to prove plenary inspiration by appealing to the character of its witnesses. The appeal is two-fold. Warfield insists that he does not "assume inspiration in order to prove inspiration" ("Inspiration and Criticism" 399-400). But he does contend that we must take seriously the claims of the biblical writers to be speaking for God. "If a sober and honest writer claims to be inspired by God, then here, at least, is a phenomenon to be accounted for" (400). He also appeals to the authority of Christ: "We believe this doctrine of the plenary inspiration of the Scriptures primarily because it is the doctrine which Christ and his apostles believed, and which they have taught us" ("Inspiration" 74). It is not necessary to search the Gospels for Christ's defense of plenary inspiration, because no such defense exists. But fundamentalists claim that Christ's citations of the Old Testament — the entire scripture of his day — are validation of its verbal inspiration, and by extrapolation, endorsement of the inspiration of the New Testament yet to be written.[7]

Fundamentalist resistance to an historico-critical approach to the biblical text — what was once called the "higher criticism" — is buttressed by their view of Christ's authority. It is maintained, for example, that the whole of Isaiah must have been written by Isaiah; otherwise Christ was in error when, citing Isa. 53.1, he referred to "Esaias the prophet" in John 12.38, or John interpolated the error himself (Lindsell 101-02; Payne 104). Similarly, the editors of the *New Scofield Reference Bible* make a point of glossing Jesus's references to the scriptures: e.g., "Our Lord here affirms the historicity and inspiration of Exod. 3" (note to Mark 12.26); "The Lord Jesus Christ here affirms both the Davidic authorship and the inspiration of Ps. 110" (note to Mark 12.36). Fundamentalists find source criticism particularly appalling, not only because it appears to conflict with the Bible's self-testimony, but because it appears to cast doubt on the perfect knowledge and authority of Jesus.

J. I. Packer expends considerable energy attempting to demonstrate Christ's high regard for the scriptures and his personal subordination thereto (54-62). Not for a moment would he agree with Herbert Schneidau's well-supported thesis that the Bible "corrects and reshapes its own verbal formulas. The motto for this function would be the refrain of the Sermon on the Mount: 'ye have heard it said. . .but I say unto you' etc." (266). As any reader of the Gospels can attest, Christ's attitude toward the law, toward religious authority in general, is ambiguous at best. One can debate this question at greater length than I am able to do so here, but what is important for our purposes is the logic of Packer's conclusion. Having marshalled all the evidence on the side of Christ's keeping the law, he concludes:

> Christ does not judge Scripture; He obeys it and fulfils it. By word and deed He endorses the authority of the whole of it. Certainly, He is the final authority for Christians; that is precisely why Christians are bound to acknowledge the authority of Scripture. Christ teaches them to do so. (61)

Thus, the fundamentalist argument comes full circle. The "final authority" of Christ is equated to the authority of scripture. The Son of God imprints the scriptures with his divine stamp of approval; his authority is never extrinsic to the text. Although fundamentalists typically use the words "personal experience with Christ" to describe a valid salvation experience, it is clear that whatever subjective impressions or emotions one may experience in this encounter must be validated by linking them in some way to the biblical text — which, unlike human experience, is always inerrant.

Although I and the fundamentalists I am citing have used extant copies of scriptural texts, and English translations at that, to illustrate the inerrancy doctrine, fundamentalists claim that inerrancy is properly an attribute only of the lost autographs. I quote Article X of the Chicago Statement in full:

> We affirm that inspiration, strictly speaking, applies only to the autographic text of Scripture, which in the providence of God can be ascertained from available manuscripts with great accuracy. We further affirm that copies and translations of Scripture are the Word of God to the extent that they faithfully represent the original.

> We deny that any essential element of the Christian faith is affected by the absence of the autographs. We further deny that this absence renders the assertion of Biblical inerrancy invalid or irrelevant. (Geisler 496)

This denial is justified in the succeeding "Exposition" in two ways. First, it is noted that "God has nowhere promised an inerrant transmission of Scripture" (501). Thus one is not obliged to maintain that copies are inerrant. Second, it is acknowledged that "no translation is or can be perfect" (502). Thus, one cannot properly ascribe inerrancy to translations. But the Council follows Torrey's virtual inerrancy model by observing that original language copies "appear to be amazingly well preserved" and that "English-speaking Christians, at least, are exceedingly well-served in these days with a host of excellent translations and have no cause for hesitating to conclude that the true Word of God is within their reach" (501-02). The Council does not address why God did not more carefully superintend the transmission and translation of his word, although the general verdict among fundamentalists is that such a question is both unanswerable and inadmissible. As Greg L. Bahnsen admonishes, "In the long run, however, we simply have to turn away from such questions, which presume to have an a priori idea of what to expect from God" (182).

Both James Barr and Dewey Beegle have written well-reasoned and thorough critiques of biblical inerrancy, and each focuses on the ambiguities and internal contradictions of the doctrine. Both argue that the phenomena of the biblical text itself prove inerrancy to be a warrantless and theologically unnecessary attribute of the text, and to defend inerrancy necessarily results in strained, illogical and biased interpretations. While Barr has no logical difficulty with the notion of verbal inspiration, saying, "if the verbal form of the Bible were different, then its meaning would be different" (287), his critique can be summarized by noting that he does not understand why fundamentalists do not then admit to dictation, a position which would at least make logical sense (290). Beegle covers much of the same ground, but briefly discusses why verbal inspiration is ultimately of little use in interpretation, saying that "Scripture is no exception to [the] linguistic fact" of multiple reference, the presuppositions of the interpreter, and the inability of language to carry the full freight of intended meaning (239-40).

Christ's attitude toward scripture is indeed one of reverence, says Beegle, but "the prevailing tendency of Jewish interpretation, to stress the letter instead of the spirit of the law, is the very thing Jesus is refuting in Matthew 5:17-48" (216). Barr argues that it is ridiculous to assume on the part of Jesus any competence or interest in historico-critical questions posed nineteen centuries hence, and agrees that such passages as the Sermon on the Mount demonstrate quite clearly that Christ "had something to say of his own that went beyond" but not necessarily against the law (81-82).

Fundamentalist protestations to the contrary, it seems obvious that attribution of inerrancy only to lost autographs renders the inerrancy claim inponderable, because of the impossibility of verification, and useless, because there is no practical value to the interpreter. It further seems obvious that the autographs serve as a convenient dodge, allowing the fundamentalist to uphold the doctrine in the face of textual evidence to its contrary. And Beegle makes two other important observations. As I have noted, Beegle too sees that textual errors are evils incompatible with the nature of God, and accordingly the fundamentalist must resort to the nonexistent autographs "to protect the honor and perfection of God" (156). Beegle also notes a fact most damning to the fundamentalist conception of inerrancy:

> Probably most of what Jesus said in public and to his disciples was in Aramaic. But the *inspired original Gospels were written in Greek*; that is, the *autographs* of the Gospels *were translations* for the most part. Consistency would mean denying the Gospels the rank of inspired Scripture, but no one has dared follow the inference to its ultimate conclusion. (169)

Why, given compelling evidence to the contrary, do fundamentalists insist the Bible is inerrant, even as they so waffle on the term *inerrancy* that it sometimes appears they do not believe in it either? It is here that J. I. Packer contributes to the discussion. *"Fundamentalism" and the Word of God* is barely concerned with specific textual problems; it is instead a theoretical defense of inerrancy, its main contention being that without inerrancy, there can be no authority. For Packer, authority is clear and unambiguous: the words *objectivity, certainty, reason,* and *science* recur throughout the work. Packer claims that "subjectivism in any form is incompatible with Christianity" (153). Christian faith appears to be little more than holy philosophy, a matter of believing the right things:

> Modern man, sceptical and indifferent as he is to dogmatic pronouncements about the supernatural order, may find it hard to take seriously the idea that one's eternal welfare may depend on what one believes; but the apostles were sure that it was so. Theological error was to them a grim reality, as was the spiritual shipwreck which comes in its wake. (43)

Everything smacking of subjectivity — the Holy Spirit, prayer, one's emotions during worship — is subordinated to the biblical text. The Holy Spirit, the third person of the Trintiy, is like Christ made a handmaiden of the text:

> the Holy Spirit, who caused [the Bible] to be written, has been given
> to the Church to cause believers to recognize it for the divine Word
> that it is, and to enable them to interpret it rightly and understand
> its meaning. (47)

It is impossible for the fundamentalist to deny the agency of the Holy Spirit,
but clearly someone as nebulous and unverifiable as the Holy Spirit must
be carefully reined, lest he break the bonds of the text. While some
fundamentalists, i.e., Pentecostals and charismatics, do place great emphasis
on the work of the Holy Spirit in the believer's life, Packer's portrait is
not uncommon in fundamentalist literature. The Holy Spirit is a helpful
librarian leading one to the text, the inner light a reading lamp illuminating
the pages of scripture.

Packer's emphasis on the word extends as well to privileging word
over deed. Revelation is not God's acts, not holy history: "the mighty acts
of God are not revelation to man at all, except in so far as they are
accompanied by words of God to explain them" (92). It is not surprising
then that Packer chooses the most doctrinal book of the New Testament —
Romans — as "the fittest starting-point for biblical interpretation and
theology" (107). Packer makes it explicit that the work of Christ, and the
paramount act of his atoning death, could not be known without the
explanations of Paul and his colleagues. "Whoever could have *guessed*,
without being told, that the man Jesus was God incarnate . . . that by
dying a criminal's death He put away the sins of mankind?" (92).[8]

This is a reasonable point, but it also illustrates how thoroughly fundamentalists privilege verbalization. Moreover, as soon as one engages in
interpreting a difficult text — which the Bible surely is, especially when
conceived of as one coherent text rather than an anthology of sixty-six
texts — disagreements among interpreters inevitably arise. Such great
literary works as the plays of Shakespeare have generated no end of
interpretation and controversy. We have come to expect this dynamic as
a normal one, and indeed we christen it as evidence of the worthiness
of a text. The simple text, the perspicuous work, rarely finds a prominent
place in the canon of western literature.

By definition, however, the Bible is for the fundamentalist the ultimate
repository of truth. Textually generated controversy cannot therefore be
blamed on the ambiguity of the text; the fault must lie with the ineptitude
or moral error of the interpreter. Thus it is not surprising that fundamentalism is characterized by frequent and bitter doctrinal disputes, as we shall
shortly see.

In sum, fundamentalists regard the inerrancy of the biblical text as
vital to authority. But because fallible readers interpret the infallible text,

the efficacy of an inerrant text is called into question. To guard against vagaries in interpretation, there must be rules and strategies for reading the infallible text. The most notorious of these is "taking the Bible literally" — the subject of the next chapter.

Chapter 4

For Reproof:
Literal Sense(s)

To say that verbal meaning is determinate is not to exclude complexities of meaning but only to insist that a text's meaning is what it is and not a hundred other things.

E. D. Hirsch[1]

Once the institution licenses a text for full-scale exegetical exploitation there is no limit.

Frank Kermode[2]

Ask anyone what distinguishes fundamentalist interpretation from that of other Bible readers, and you are likely to be told that fundamentalists take the Bible literally. Asked what that means, fundamentalist and non-fundamentalist alike will agree that literalistic reading is based on "common sense," with "hidden" or "deeper" meanings rejected in favor of the "plain" or "obvious" sense. For example, in *God, Revelation and Authority*, Carl F. H. Henry states, "The rule among evangelicals is to follow the natural meaning of a Scriptural text" (4.104).

Literalism is an attempt, it seems to me, to guard against the vagaries of those perverse interpreters who would persist in making a text mean "a hundred other things." As those who have taught freshman literature can attest, one will often encounter resistance (expressed in the formulaic assertion that the professor or a student reader is "finding stuff in the story that isn't there") to interpretations other than those which reflect the patently obvious. While some students delight in such discoveries, others are frustrated by English studies, disturbed by its ambiguities and by the consequent refusal of most English professors to say there is a single *right* way of interpreting a text. Because English students need not worry about the salvation of their souls, however, multiplexity of interpretation is still far less disquieting for them than it is for fundamentalists.

We would not go far wrong in saying that literalistic reading practices are virtually synonymous with the common reader's approach to a text, when that approach is unencumbered by notions of what one *ought* to find in that text. In ordinary parlance, *literal* is a virtual synonym for *sensible*, and I have fully in mind here both the connotations of "reasonable" and "apprehensible by the senses." While common sense is a virtue much cherished by the American mind — one cannot help thinking, ironically, of Thomas Paine, whose appeal to that very virtue helped foster the American Revolution — it nevertheless happens that my commonsensical reading of a biblical passage might strike someone else as obtuse, nonsensical, heretical or any combination of these adjectives. Given, however, that fundamentalism defends my right to read the "plain book" for myself, it is, paradoxically, in a literalistic approach to scripture that the greatest evidence of "full-scale exegetical exploitation" is to be found. Fundamentalism hopes to ensure orthodoxy by appealing to "the literal truth of an inerrant Bible" (Henry 4.122), yet when hundreds of thousands of readers are following their own common sense, it becomes woefully apparent that such sense is not so "common" after all.

We will first analyze some examples of literalistic reading, with special attention given to *dispensationalist* interpretations. Of those fundamentalists who themselves claim to take the Bible literally, the vast majority are dispensationalists, indebted to the early twentieth-century Bible editor and scholar, C. I. Scofield, who in turn is indebted to J. N. Darby, a mid–nineteenth-century English nonconformist.[3] While Darby is generally acknowledged as the creator of fundamentalist dispensationalism, it was C. I. Scofield who popularized the scheme, particularly through his enormously influential annotated edition of the King James Version (first edition 1909). The *New Scofield Reference Bible*, published in 1967, well after Scofield's death, represents the work of a committee of dispensationalist commentators.

Dispensationalism provides a distinctive way of interpreting the Bible as a whole and its apocalyptic passages in particular. Its eschatology arises from a "literal" reading of the books of Daniel and Revelation in the sense that these apocalyptic writings are believed to foretell actual events in the future. Because Scofield believes that the Bible reports fulfillments of prophecy, he asserts that prophecies as yet unfulfilled must likewise literally come to pass:

> Of these seven promises to Mary [found in Luke 1] *five* have already been *literally* fulfilled. By what rule of interpretation are we authorized to say that the remaining two will not be also fulfilled? (*Rightly Dividing the Word of Truth* 14-15)

Another dispensationalist, Oliver B. Greene, shares Scofield's appeal to "literal" historical events in support of his literalist eschatology:

Jesus died a literal death. He was buried — not figuratively or spiritually, but *literally*, in a literal tomb. And He literally rose again — bodily, as He had declared He would and as it had been prophesied. (314)

Despite these clarion calls for literalistic interpretation, however, fundamentalists often do not interpret passages according to their literal, obvious sense. Consider another exegesis from *Rightly Dividing the Word of Truth*. Concerning John 5.28-29, a passage about the resurrection of both the good and the evil, Scofield remarks:

If it be objected that the word "hour" would indicate a *simultaneous* resurrection of these two classes, it is answered that the "hour" of verse 25 has already lasted eighteen hundred years. (39)

The "hour" of John 5.25, not incidentally, is spoken by Jesus in this context:

Verily, verily, I say unto you, The hour is coming, and now is, when the dead shall hear the voice of the Son of God: and they that hear shall live.

Here of course, Scofield is dodging a familiar problem — what would seem to be Jesus's erroneous proclamation of imminent apocalypse — by using historical fact to validate his interpretation. That Jesus may have been mistaken or speaking figuratively is, for Scofield, impious and unthinkable. In this passage, Scofield further observes how the word *day* is used in such verses as 2 Peter 3.8 to support his arguably non-literal interpretation of the word *hour*. Second Peter 3.8, it should be noted, has furnished many literally-minded prophesiers with grist for chronologies. The verse reads:

But, beloved, be not ignorant of this one thing, that one day is with the Lord as a thousand years, and a thousand years as one day.

The non-canonical Epistle of Barnabas, noting the world was created in six days, infers that it will *end* in six days, i.e., six thousand years. Evangelist Jack van Impe's similar disregard for simile enabled him to imply, in his *Signs of the Times* (1979), that the world would end in 1982 (64-66).

It is becoming apparent already that the intrusion of theological presuppositions — presuppositions which are claimed to be grounded in literalistic interpretation — will in fact militate against the literal sense of certain passages. Conversely, even literalists who share the same theology and eschatology will arrive at markedly different interpretations of the same passage. As illustration, it is fruitful to consider what Oliver Greene, Leon I. Bates (another populist evangelist), and the phenomenally successful author Hal Lindsey, make of Rev. 9.13-19. The text itself reads:

> And the sixth angel sounded, and I heard a voice from the four horns of the golden altar which is before God. Saying to the sixth angel which had the trumpet, Loose the four angels which are bound in the great river Euphrates. And the four angels were loosed, which were prepared for an hour, and a day, and a month, and a year, for to slay the third part of men. And the number of the army of the horsemen were two hundred thousand thousand: and I heard the number of them. And thus I saw the horses in the vision, and them that sat on them, having breastplates of fire, and of jacinth, and brimstone: and the heads of the horses were as the heads of lions; and out of their mouths issued fire and smoke and brimstone. By these three was the third part of men killed, by the fire, and by the smoke, and by the brimstone, which issued out of their mouths. For their power is in their mouth, and in their tails: for their tails were like unto serpents, and had heads, and with them they do hurt.

Greene comments:

> It would be unreasonable to interpret the army of two hundred million horsemen under the sixth trumpet as being anything *other* than supernatural because, in the first place, it would be literally impossible to gather that many horses for military use even if all the horses in the world were accessible for that purpose. In the second place, we know this will be an army of supernatural creatures because the horses are described as having heads "as the heads of lions" and tails "like unto serpents, and had heads." (159)

Note first that when the literal would necessarily involve the fantastic or the empirically impossible, Greene does not hesitate to replace literal, i.e., "real," horses and horsemen with supernatural ones. That Greene even feels compelled to make this remark about a passage so obviously rich in poetic imagery reveals a certain anxiety about any departure from the literalism principle. And in any case, he insists upon the literal occurrence of this battle, vigorously opposing throughout *The Second Coming of Christ* any attempt to allegorize or spiritualize the book of Revelation. He also makes a point of disregarding simile: these are not natural horses notable for their ferocity or even their shaggy manes, but supernatural beasts. Thus, the inability to countenance poetic imagery and a belief in literal reference result necessarily in interpreting this passage as descriptive of supernatural creatures.

But while Greene's horses emerge from a supernatural stable, Bates's horses are termed "vehicles," and those destroyed:

> will be killed by the FIRE, SMOKE and PROJECTILES (missiles?) being issued out of the vehicles upon which the army is riding (Rev. 9:17, 18). *Could John have been trying to describe modern, missile launching TANKS?* (159)

Bates shows even less regard for the literal sense of the words of this passage, preferring to advance an interpretation in keeping with present-day possibilities. While supernatural intervention is certainly not absent from Bates's exegesis, he does not feel at all constrained by the syntax to postulate supernatural creatures; he interprets the passage as symbolic of human artifices. Most interestingly, however, Bates will freely combine creative translation of biblical signifier to modern signified with the most stubborn literalism:

> Since 1964, Red China has reportedly had a 200,000,000 armed and organized militia. This is the EXACT NUMBER predicted in God's Word. **Coincidence? Not likely!** (113)

Red China is, of course, not mentioned by name in the scriptures; nevertheless, Bates feels free to make such a non-literal inference while at the same time refusing to acknowledge that 200,000,000 might be a round number, whether rounded by St. John or modern journalists.

Finally, Hal Lindsey, whose *The Late Great Planet Earth*, published in 1970, has sold over 18 million copies (Weber 211), has this to say about our text:

> The phenomena by which this destruction of life will take place is given: it will be by fire, smoke (or air pollution), and brimstone (or melted earth). The thought may have occurred to you that this is strikingly similar to the phenomena associated with thermonuclear war. In fact, many Bible expositors [Lindsey does not say who] believe that this is an accurate first-century description of a twentieth-century thermonuclear war. (82)

These three interpretations, taken together, present a rather disconcerting triptych not only of dispensationalism but of "literalism." Three interpreters,

closely allied in theology and methodology, have progressed from supernatural beasts to "missile launching tanks" all the way to thermonuclear
warfare. *Horses* can signify supernatural horse-like creatures, tanks, or
nuclear warheads — but each interpreter nonetheless holds to an inerrantist
(and literalist) view of the text. If, as I proposed at the beginning of this
chapter, literalism seeks to save us from contradiction and proliferation
of interpretations, it here at least does nothing of the kind. On the contrary, the text seems to have been, in Kermode's words, "licensed for full-
scale exegetical exploitation."

And it is in this exploitation that one frequently finds the excesses and
naiveties of interpretation characteristic of literalism run amok. Regarding
Rev. 9.11, which says that a judgmental horde of locusts has a king, Greene
remarks, "This army of demon-locusts is *organized* — they have a king.
Ordinary locusts of the earth have no king (Prov. 30:27)" (156). Greene
is following common fundamentalist practice in giving supporting scriptural
citations parenthetically, but the full impact of this moment will be lost,
I fear, unless I quote Prov. 30.27 myself: "The locusts have no king, yet
go they forth all of them by bands." (This verse occurs within a short
discourse on exemplary animals "little" yet "exceeding wise." The full
context is 30.24-28.) Comical as it is, Greene's exegesis reveals two important interpretive presuppositions held often enough by dispensationalist
and non-dispensationalist alike: 1) any given passage of scripture can shed
light on any other given passage, and 2) the Bible is a repository of
rational propositions and empirical information. The writer of the Proverbs
passage is not merely giving a moral lesson in the manner of Aesop; he
is giving us a lesson in the sociobiology of locusts. Bates also comments
on the locusts of Revelation, agreeing with Greene as to their literality.
As is his wont though, Bates will find a contemporary, empirical application. Given "their faces like men and hair like women," Bates infers, "Many
MEN now have long hair like women! There has also been a tremendous
increase of homosexual, female impersonators" (157).

Fundamentalist and non-fundamentalist scholars alike may be tempted
to state that neither Greene nor Bates is very bright, and indeed it is a
spacious leap from the comparative exegetical restraint of a Scofield to
the speculations of a Bates. Although Bates's frequent boldfacing, exclama-
tion points, and capitalization of entire words are traditional tip-offs to sen-
sationalism, one cannot make premature evaluations of this material on
the basis of offensive typography. Until we investigate how fundamental
hermeneutical principles generate such interpretations, we cannot summarily dismiss them as naive or extremist.

Those familiar with James Barr's *Fundamentalism* will know that Barr
has provided compelling arguments against viewing fundamentalist inter-

pretation as literalistic, in part because he restricts his own study to analysis of relatively scholarly evangelicals.[4] Because the literal sense of many passages threatens the doctrine of biblical inerrancy, Barr argues that inerrancy is regnant: "Inerrancy is maintained only by constantly altering the mode of interpretation, and in particular by abandoning the literal sense as soon as it would be an embarrassment to the view of inerrancy held" (46). In discussing how a "symbolic and non-literal interpretation" of Genesis 1 is now "preferred" by fundamentalists, Barr notes that "it is now only very extreme fundamentalists who assert that a literal interpretation of the six days of creation is obligatory, or even desirable" (42). Barr further contends that critical biblical scholarship, most of it anathema to fundamentalists, is far more literalistic in its hermeneutics than is fundamentalism. Source criticism of the Pentateuch — the postulation of several sources for these books rather than sole Mosaic authorship — is, according to Barr, the result of taking these texts literally. Source critics "did not allow defensive and harmonizing interpretations to push aside the literal sense of the text" (47).

Although Barr's analysis is correct, as far as it goes, it trades on an equivocation all too common both in fundamentalism itself and in studies of the phenomenon. There are two senses of the word *literalism*. On the one hand, it can be taken to mean the disallowance of figurative or symbolic interpretation: horses are always horses, never tanks or warheads. On the other hand, *literal* also denotes the empirical or the ostensively referential. One need not believe that actual fire and brimstone will spew from the mouths of actual horses, whether natural or supernatural, in order to believe that an empirically sensible invasion of death-dealing forces will actually take place at some point in the future. It is important to understand that whatever Greene's and Bates's disagreement on particulars, neither would accept the notion that the details of Revelation are in any way allegorical or "merely" symbolic.

One finds, moreover, evidence of literalism — and unwitting equivocation, perhaps — in the work of those purporting only to defend biblical inerrancy. In *The Battle for the Bible,* immediately after denying that inerrantists are " 'wooden-headed literalists' " (37), Harold Lindsell offers an amazingly wooden reading of Job 38.7, in which God rhetorically asks Job where he was "When the morning stars sang together, and all the sons of God shouted for joy?". Lindsell comments:

> In Job 38:7 the morning stars are said to sing together. That sounds far-fetched and it has even been thought of as figurative language. But scientists now tell us that in the air there is music that comes from the stars. (38)

Such a reading does support Barr's contention that biblical inerrancy is the central issue in fundamentalism, and further that the fundamentalist conception of truth is grounded in "correspondence to external reality" (49).[5] But would the singing stars of Job be "erroneous" if scientists had not discovered sounds emanating from the stars? If not — if it is indeed irrelevant to ascribe error to figurative language — why does Lindsell feel compelled to remark on the literality of star sounds? For Lindsell, it is clear that the literal sense of scripture is part and parcel of inerrancy. His dismissal of a figurative interpretation further reflects the belief that literal reference is of higher value than the merely figurative.

In the same way, one will find vehement insistence on the literality of such biblical figures as Adam and Eve, and Jonah. Francis Schaeffer's *No Final Conflict* is a short work arguing for the historicity of the entire book of Genesis and the human existence of individuals named Adam and Eve. While not using the word *literal*, he contends "that Genesis is history and that it is to be read in normal fashion, with the common use of the words and syntax" (18). This emphasis on the "normal" and the "common" is certainly equivalent to asking one to "take the Bible literally," in the ordinary meaning of that phrase. As for Adam and Eve, Schaeffer cites Paul's references to Adam, especially in 1 Corinthians, as supporting the historicity of the first couple, and concludes too

> that Genesis itself emphasizes strongly that Adam was a historic character. We read in Genesis 4:1, "And Adam knew Eve his wife; and she conceived, and bare Cain, and said, I have gotten a man from the LORD." This verse is *meaningless* unless both Adam and Eve as well as the birth of the child are taken to be historic. (21, emphasis added).

Lindsell agrees, explicitly equating the belief that Adam and Eve are mythical with belief that the Bible is erroneous (80). Unless these characters are literal, i.e., historical, figures, it is maintained that the stories in which they appear are erroneous, untrue, and meaningless.

It is important to note how closely the plausibility of the *literal* sense of biblical passages is linked to maintaining the inerrancy of the text. It will not suffice to claim that we have simply been confused in attributing literalism to fundamentalists. Our examples have shown that a tendency toward literalism is evident even in "evangelical" literature.

The power of fundamentalist hermeneutics is, in part, based on its appeal to ostensive reference and the empirically sensible, what Hans Frei, in *The Eclipse of Biblical Narrative* calls a "precritical realistic reading" of the Bible (2). Frei's study is concerned with English and German biblical hermeneutics of the eighteenth and nineteenth centuries, focusing on conflicts between "lower" and "higher" critics, a situation strikingly parallel to the conflict between contemporary American fundamentalists and mainstream Protestants. As Frei demonstrates, literal reference is strongly liked to the *historicity* of an account. Biblical narratives are indisputably "realistic" and "history-like;" given their character, one is quite naturally compelled to ask if they are therefore true (16).

Thus, when fundamentalists champion the truth of scripture, they do so by exploiting the popular assumption that myths or fables cannot be "true." Similarly, their literalistic interpretation of tropes reflects the even more popular assumption that the concrete sense of a passage is its true sense. Fire and brimstone are exactly that, not mere metaphors for the wrath of God:

> Ask an Evangelical whether or not he believes there are flames in hell, and after a thirty-minute philosophical recitation on the theological implications of eternal retribution in light of the implicit goodness of God, you will still not know what he really believes. Ask a Fundamentalist whether he believes there are really flames in hell and he will simply say, "Yes, and hot ones too!" This is why left-wing Evangelicalism has failed to make any substantial use of the media. It cannot express its theology in the concrete terminology of television English. (Falwell, ed. 172)

Although one may find the sense of humor in this passage to be rather warped, literal hellfire serving as material for flip remarks, this passage also illustrates the power of literalism: making the obligatory swipe at philosophical eggheads, it then appeals to one's ability to visualize and to feel imaginatively the horrible fate of unbelievers. It is this power of imagery which is the poet's stock in trade; consider that an abstract essay on the problem of evil could not begin to approach the emotional power of Blake's "The Chimney Sweeper" (in *Songs of Experience*), with its depiction of a wretched child condemned to arduous labor, his parents " 'gone to praise God & his Priest & King,/Who make up a heaven of our misery.' "

Although a literalistic approach is not necessarily in opposition to figural interpretation — one can, for example, practice the letter of the law by practicing circumcision and at the same time acknowledge, with Paul, the greater importance of a figural circumcision of the heart (Rom. 2.29) — there is no reason, once one arrives in the New Testament, to interpret in any way but literally.

One might also define the literal sense of words contextually if we consider context to include one's preconception of a text. According to

Stephen W. Paine, one of the translators of the New International Version, it was required of all NIV translators that they "believe in the inerrancy of Scripture" (2). The presupposition of scriptural inerrancy governs the choices of translators, as Paine describes in this instructive example:

> Suppose you did not believe that the Bible was inerrant, the word of God, that it was just an ancient book with a lot of good ideas that should be preached, but that's it. Then when something like Isaiah 7:14 comes up where *young woman* [RSV; an oft-cited reason for burning this translation] and *virgin* [KJV] are juxtaposed, if you didn't believe in actual bona fide predictive prophecy in the Bible, you'd have an excellent chance to vote 'young woman' and your reasons for it would be clear — and it could have been put either way without violating the Hebrew. But when in the New Testament you come to the same passage in Matthew, but in Greek, if you believe in the inerrancy of Scripture, you have to believe that Matthew correctly reproduced Isaiah and came out with the Greek word which means only virgin. (2)

Thus the authority of any modern translation is determined by the authority of the translators; that is, do they or do they not subscribe to the fundamentalist doctrines of scripture? Paine's example is interesting too in that it evinces defense of a watershed doctrine; the virgin birth of Christ is a "test case" by which fundamentalist orthodoxy is determined (Barr 176). The doctrine has little theological or imaginative value in fundamentalism, as both Barr and Stewart Cole have observed (Barr 176; Cole 329). It is, rather, a doctrine in Foucault's sense of that word — "the sign, the manifestation and the instrument of a prior adherence" (*Discourse* 226). Its function is to indicate one's fidelity to the discourse. But although the inerrancy doctrine does make Paine's translation decision clear, it does not cause him to abandon regard for the letter. Paine is much concerned with the literal sense of Isa. 7.14; his difficulty arises with translating a Hebrew word of potentially multiple reference. A text may have more than one literal meaning, Stanley Fish has shown, because the literal, "obvious" sense of a text will change in accordance with its placement in context.[6]

Although the presupposition of textual inerrancy governs Paine's translation, one cannot infer that he is engaging in crafty manipulation of the text to prop up his doctrine of it. As Fish points out, our interpretations are rarely, if ever, free of presuppositions about the nature of the text before us: a reader of *Lycidas*, for example, proceeds in his or her interpretation with the knowledge that Milton is the author and the poem is a pastoral (168). Similarly, Paine knows that God is the ultimate author of the text before him and he knows the text is inerrant. If this seems a false analogy, one can note Fish's observation that "the notions 'pastoral' and 'Milton' are also interpretations; that is, they do not stand for a set of indisputable, objective facts; if they did, a great many books would not now be getting written" (168).

We have been accustomed, for the most part rightly, to thinking that Christians read the Old Testament figurally and allegorically. In *The Slayers of Moses*, Susan Handelman observes that in Christian interpretation the spirit of the law triumphs over the letter (14–16 and *passim*) — or as Paul himself said, "not of the letter, but of the spirit: for the letter killeth, but the spirit giveth life" (2. Cor. 3.6b). Where Christianity, in Hellenistic fashion, spiritualizes, generalizes and abstracts (86–87), Judaism particularizes, investigating the letter as the world itself in accordance with the famous midrash, "God looked into the Torah and created the world" (101). In contrast to Christianity, the canon is not closed; the Torah is, finally, both itself and its interpretations, not a text completed once for all, but "a continuous and unified process" (39).

Protestant fundamentalists do close the canon — with a resounding slam calculated to drown out the noises of tongues-speakers and others claiming direct revelation from God. But there exists, nevertheless, an effective canonicity of commentary, particularly in the case of the *Scofield Reference Bible*. It seems inevitable that the higher the status of the text, the higher the status of commentary thereupon, and in this sense fundamentalist interpretation may be more rabbinical than priestly.[7] The Scofield Bible is heavily typological in its interpretation of the Old Testament, yet this "spiritualizing" of the scriptures is not, as Handelman would maintain, contradictory of literalistic interpretation so much as it is derivative of literalism. Such interpretation has been a necessary consequence of the *kerygma* — Christ's proclamation of a new gospel — coupled with the need to maintain the divine authority of the old testament upon which the new testament is founded. As Frank Kermode observes in *The Genesis of Secrecy*, "The entire Jewish Bible was to be sacrificed to the validation of the historicity of the gospels; yet its whole authority was needed to establish that historicity" (107). We can also apply Hans Frei's analysis to contemporary fundamentalist interpretation:

> Far from being in conflict with the literal sense of biblical stories, figuration or typology was a natural extension of literal interpretation. It was literalism at the level of the whole biblical story and thus of the depiction of the whole of historical reality. (2)

Conservative eighteenth and nineteenth century interpretations of biblical prophecy are strikingly prefigurative of the methodology of Darby-Scofield dispensationalism, the continuing influence of which is not quite as restricted as Frei thinks:

> The doctrine of emphasis and the experimentation with the reference of numerical schemes to events in the overarching world of common history disappeared soon enough from responsible scholarship, although both have remained standard ploys in Christian folk piety. (178–79)

While Frei does not define "folk piety," it seems amply established that contemporary adherents to this method of biblical interpretation are not just a few simple-minded folk living in geographical and intellectual backwaters. Although not all fundamentalists are dispensationalists, the dispensational "depiction of the whole of historical reality" has no serious rivals in fundamentalist circles.

The dispensational scheme is intricate and ingenious: Barr has called it "a remarkable achievement of the mythopoeic fantasy," saying it "might well compare with the apocalyptic poems of Blake" (195). According to Scofield, the biblical text is to be divided into seven distinct dispensations or ages (*Rightly Dividing* 18–23; see also *Scofield Reference Bible*):

I. Innocence [before the Fall]
II. Conscience [between the Fall and the Flood; begins Gen. 1.23]
III. Human Government [between the Flood and Babel; begins Gen. 8.20]
IV. Promise [inaugurated by the call of Abraham; begins Gen. 12.1]
V. Law [inaugurated by the giving of the Law to Moses; begins Exod. 19.8]
VI. Grace [inaugurated by the death of Christ; begins Matt. 27.51 with the rending of the temple veil, and at corresponding points in the other gospels; this is the present dispensation.]
VII. Personal Reign of Christ [commences with the Second Coming; not marked in the biblical text, but roughly Rev. 19.]

Scofield distinguishes the dispensations by discovering in each case "some change in God's method of dealing with mankind. . . . Each of the dispensations may be regarded as a new test of the natural man, and each ends in judgment — marking his utter failure in every dispensation" (*Rightly Dividing* 18).

The first four dispensations need not concern us here, but the last three are of great importance both to dispensationalists themselves and to those examining how their Bible reading functions. There are three aspects of dispensationalism I want to discuss with regard to investigating its interpretive authority: the status of the gospel texts, resolution of intertextual contradiction, and premillennialist eschatology.

The present dispensation, that of grace, begins not with the birth or even the earthly ministry of Christ, but with his *death*. It is maintained that Christ lives and teaches during the now-obsolete dispensation of law. Consequently, one must ask a rather startling question: are the words and teachings of Christ himself relevant to Christians? Consider Scofield's gloss on Luke 11.1. Although Scofield calls the Lord's Prayer "an incomparable model," he asserts:

> Used as a *form*, the Lord's prayer is, dispensationally, upon legal, not church ground; it is not a prayer in the name of Christ (cf. John 14.13, 14; 16.24); and it makes human forgiveness, as under the law it must, the condition of divine forgiveness; an order which grace exactly reverses (cf. Eph. 4.32).

It seems a proper inference that the excellence of the Lord's Prayer as a "model" notwithstanding, actually to *pray* this prayer is illegitimate. What is the status of other words of Christ? What of, say, the Sermon on the Mount? In his preface to "The Four Gospels" (in the *Reference Bible*), Scofield comments, "The mission of Jesus was, *primarily*, to the Jews (Mt. 10.5, 6; 15.23–25; John 1.11)." Thus, "The Sermon on the Mount is law, not grace, for it demands as the condition of blessing (Mt. 5. 3–9) that perfect character which grace, through divine power, creates (Gal. 5.22, 23)." Scofield goes on to note:

> The *doctrines* of grace are to be sought in the Epistles, not in the Gospels; but those doctrines rest back upon the death and resurrection of Christ, and upon the great germ-truths to which He gave utterance, and of which the Epistles are the unfolding. Furthermore, the only perfect example of perfect grace is the Christ of the Gospels.

Thus, the words of Christ — found in the Gospel texts — are relegated to a secondary role in dispensationalism, and the writings of Paul in particular assume primary status. In short, the main significance of Christ is to be found in the act of his death, not in the "germ-truths" of his utterances. I shall not elaborate on the strictly theological implications here, although it is generally agreed among Christians who trouble to criticize dispensationalism at all that this devaluation of Christ's teachings is a serious error.[8] While this study is not concerned with heresy as a theological matter, it is concerned with how fundamentalist authorities manage the text: the Pauline writings are central to fundamentalist interpretation, a centrality possibly traceable to dispensationalism.

By drawing the line between law and grace *after* Christ's earthly ministry, dispensationalists have succeeded in resolving numerous apparent contradictions between the teachings of Christ and those of Paul. By using the dispensational scheme, one is no longer faced with any difficulty reconciling these two representative New Testament passages: "Not every one that saith unto me, Lord, Lord, shall enter into the kingdom of heaven; but he that doeth the will of my Father which is in heaven" (Matt. 7.21) and "For whosoever shall call upon the name of the Lord shall be saved" (Rom. 10.13). Once we understand, with Scofield, that Jesus was speaking in and through the age of law, Jesus's apparent requirement of good works for salvation is quite comprehensible: put another way, he was not really addressing Christians. Even Barr manages some faint praise for dispensationalists' effort to cope with textual difficulties:

> The whole dispensational framework is in a certain mad way an attempt to cope with problems and facts that were being dealt with by critical study at the same time in a completely different mental world. Dispensationalism gives some sort of recognition, however distorted, to the fact that what Jesus says is not the same as what Paul says. (198)

But it is the dispensationalist scenario of the "Last Days" that is its best known feature.[9] Dispensationalists are premillennialists, believing that the decline of world civilization is inevitable and imminent.[10] As Sandeen has shown, literalism and premillennialism are parallel and mutually dependent phenomena (107–111). Certainly it is impossible for one to be a postmillennialist or amillennialist and take apocalyptic passages of scripture literally. The terrible judgments of Revelation must refer either figuratively to past events or allegorically to the ongoing conflict between good and evil. Premillennialists believe the literal, historical deterioration of the earth will culminate in a seven-year period of *tribulation*, the horrific details of which are culled from the books of Daniel and Revelation. The tribulation, an outpouring of divine wrath and judgment, will close with the second coming of Christ, who will then reign on earth during the millennium. Believers, however, will not suffer through the tribulation. In an event termed the *rapture*, Christ will return to gather his saints from the earth immediately prior to the onset of the tribulation. They will return with Christ to reign with him on earth during the millennium. The rapture can occur at any moment; no biblical prophecies need have been fulfilled. In essence, therefore, Christ comes twice (although premillennialists do not term these events the Second and Third Coming of Christ). The Last Judgment occurs at the close of the millennium, with all persons sent to their respective eternal destinations.

The philosophical and political consequences of premillennialist thought can hardly be overstated: human efforts to effect changes for the good are not only utterly futile, but by definition contrary to the divine plan. There is, in short, literally a world of difference between one who believes that things will get better and better, and one who believes that things will get worse and worse. It is the business of the Christian to evangelize individual souls, not to engage in social or political activism. Consider, for example, this comment on Titus 2.9-10 in the *Liberty Commentary on the New Testament* (Jerry Falwell, editor): "**Servants** (Gr *doulos*) were slaves in a pagan society. Paul did not get sidetracked into social reform. One cannot transform a lost society. The gospel will transform individuals in society and this is the minister's calling." Similarly, Pat Robertson does not believe that "lasting world peace" can be achieved until Christ returns: "There is no way that a United Nations, a League of Nations, peace treaties, disarmament treaties, or any other human instrument can bring about peace"(8).[11]

It is imperative to recognize that virtually all persons who identify themselves as fundamentalists are premillennialists. Among self-identified evangelicals, premillennialism is also the majority position. In a 1987 survey of *Christianity Today* readers, 60% of those queried believe in the premillennial return of Christ; 50% believe "all prophecy should be interpreted literally" ("Our Future Hope" 9-I).

Once one comprehends premillennialist eschatology, one can more deeply appreciate the doctrinal underpinnings of the following excerpts from an editorial essay by fundamentalist Bob Jones. (Here he is attacking published Southern Baptist goals for Sunday School programs.)

> *To work for peace wherever there is war.* On the surface this sounds like a noble purpose, but the Bible tells us that there are going to be wars and rumors of wars until the Lord Jesus takes over the throne of His father David. The church is not in the world to bring peace. The gospel is a sharp, twoedged sword. Christ's commission to His disciples is to preach the gospel. . . . *To work toward a moral climate that matches the dignity of man.* The church is not told to change the moral climate of the world. The commission to the Church is to save men and women out of the world. Anybody who knows and believes the Scripture recognizes that the moral situation of the world is going to grow worse and worse as we go further and further into the apostasy.

It is vital to note that Jones appeals to knowledge and belief of the Bible as justification for opinions which many would judge inhumane and indeed unchristian. His implication is clear: "anybody who knows and believes the Scripture will agree with me." If you do not agree, you are an apostate. There is no indication in this passage, or in similar extremist premillennial writings, that Christians can disagree on the particulars of the apocalypse. By presenting a particular intepretation of the Bible as "what the Bible says," premillennialist authorities wield powerful control over the beliefs of the ordinary reader. Put another way, to disagree with Bob Jones is to disagree with the Bible is to disagree with God — hardly something one cares to do.

One can easily give plausible explanations for the appeal of premillennialism and a pretribulational rapture. One need not sacrifice one's time and money to alleviate social ills, since social problems are, in effect, God's will. Belief in an imminent rapture keeps one from having to consider one's own death. Such explanations, however, do not fully account for belief in dispensationalist eschatology. For one thing, some believers — notably children — do not find belief in an imminent rapture at all attractive. Peshkin records several statements expressing mixed feelings about the prospect. To cite one:

> I think that the time for Jesus to come is coming pretty soon. . . . It scares me because every girl wants to get married, and stuff like that, but in a way I feel bad because I know a lot of people are going to miss heaven and a lot of kids aren't going to grow up and be privileged to do things for the Lord. (215)

As Timothy Weber points out, following his consideration of the various "attractive" features of premillennialism:

> It would be too simplistic to say, however, that people become premillennialists primarily out of some kind of psychological need for security and escape. While such factors may be significant, they can hardly be considered determinative for most people. All personal reasons aside, most premillennialists accept the doctrine because they believe that the Bible teaches it. (230)

Weber is entirely correct in discerning the central role of the text in premillennialist belief. If the Bible is authoritative, and if the Bible does indeed "say" there will be a literal rapture and millennium, one is quite simply obliged to believe it. The alternative is to question the authority of the Bible. But dispensational premillennialism also affords plentiful

examples of what Kermode identifies as the feeding of "our new theoretical and methodological positions into the text; they govern the course of the narrative as it appears in our interpretation, just as, in psychoanalysis, the analyst's beliefs and procedures modify the narrative of the analysand" (*Genesis* 17). For example, Pat Robertson, describes the rise of the antichrist in these terms: "In the book of Revelation we are told that a dictator will arise from the revived Roman Empire. He will be endued with the power of Satan himself, and will take unto himself the prerogatives of God" (111). In a footnote, he directs the reader to Rev. 13. 1–18, which of course says nothing of a "revived Roman empire." That inference is a feature of dispensationalist eschatology and in fact comes from the book of Daniel. Ordinary readers may not bother to look up the reference (assuming it must be correct) nor are they likely to appreciate that Robertson's remarks are the dispensationalist *interpretation* of Revelation 13.

Biblical authority has been masterfully exploited by Hal Lindsey, author of *The Late Great Planet Earth,* a work Barr characterizes as "a farrago of nonsense" but nevertheless "little different from traditional premillennial dispensationalism" (206-07). While Weber may also be correct in suggesting that the popularity of the book reflects a purely secular appetite for the sensational and the occult (184–85), it is Lindsey's use of the biblical text — the Word of God himself — that sets his work apart from drugstore variety soothsaying.[12]

Lindsey's eschatology is far from original, but while he is clearly indebted to Darby-Scofield dispensationalism, he does not once acknowledge it. He differs from purist dispensationalism, however, in his wholesale interpretation of biblical "prophecies" as references to current events. For example, he views the 1948 statehood of Israel as confirmation of biblical passages alluding to the return of the Jewish people to their land (48–58). By contrast, the editors of the *New Scofield Reference Bible* (published in 1967) exercise considerable restraint on this matter, not once commenting on the statehood of Israel.

As the epitome of "popular" fundamentalist writing, Lindsey's work is most revealing for its convincing tone, confident authority, and compelling systematization. Lindsey achieves his effect by several means, all strongly imbued with literalistic Bible reading. The statehood of Israel, the continuing conflicts in the Middle East, the threat of nuclear war — these and many other current issues can be fit quite neatly with literalistic interpretations of the book of Revelation.

Lindsey is duly concerned with facticity, taking great pains in his early chapters to show how biblical prophets accurately foretold events in their own day. It is generally accepted among modern biblical scholars that the book of Isaiah is not authored solely by the prophet Isaiah — a later source termed "Second Isaiah" is postulated for chapters 40–66, and some scholars postulate a "Third Isaiah" for chapters 56–66. One of the consequences of this source criticism is to turn what appears superficially to be successful prophecy into history, but if one is unfamiliar with the scholarship, or rejects it, the evidence as rendered by Lindsey is compelling. In the tradition of Scofield, he then infers that prophecies yet to be fulfilled will also come literally to pass. Like all inerrantists, he strengthens his claims by infusing the miraculous with a strong dose of "science":

> Jesus' feet will first touch the earth where they left the earth, on the Mount of Olives. The mountain will split in two with a great earthquake the instant that Jesus' foot touches it. . . . It was reported to me [Lindsey does not say by whom] that an oil company doing seismic studies of this area in quest of oil discovered a gigantic fault running east and west precisely through the center of the Mount of Olives. (174)

I have twice now, in the course of quoting Lindsey, noted that his documentation of sources is virtually nonexistent. But by adopting the masterful pose of one who looks into the word of God and reveals its secrets, Lindsey manages very artfully to describe an apocalypse at once terrifying to the goats and attractive to the sheep. The terror is turned to evangelistic ends:

> Will you be here when the world is plagued by mankind's darkest day. . . ? God's Word tells us that there will be one generation of believers who will never know death. These believers will be removed from the earth before the Great Tribulation — before that period of the most ghastly pestilence, bloodshed, and starvation the world has ever known. (137–38)

And the already powerful inducement to embracing Lindsey's belief is enhanced by the knowledge that

> every believer in Jesus Christ is initiated into Christ's fraternity. Then, and only then, can he understand some of the secrets of God. These secrets the rest of the world will not accept as those who believe in Christ will accept them and understand them. (139)

On the surface, it would seem a long journey from the plain Presbyterian style of a Charles Hodge to the *National Enquirer* style of a Hal Lindsey. Yet it is clear that the biblical text plays an integral role in the theologies of both men. The moderate fundamentalist indeed finds it logically difficult to criticize anyone who confesses biblical inerrancy and literalism. J. Gresham Machen, the last of the Princeton theologians, was not a premillennialist, but he could not bring himself to condemn those who were:

> Yet how great is our agreement with those who hold the premillennial view! They share to the full our reverence for the authority of the Bible, and differ from us only in the interpretation of the Bible. (49)

The biblical text has been "licensed for full-scale exegetical exploitation." Machen is powerless to attack an eschatology he finds offensive, until he understands that "interpretation" of a text is, for all practical purposes, the text itself.

Full-scale exploitation of the text has occurred to such an extent in the last decade, in fact, that premillennialism has become submerged in political activism. The very figures who have championed fundamentalist political and social activism are themselves premillennialists, and have made no explicit repudiation of that eschatology. As late as 1984, Pat Robertson remarked on such developments as the statehood of Israel and the existence of nuclear weaponry, saying, "These things that we have brought into our lives are fulfilling biblical prophecies. . . . This is why I fully expect to be alive when Jesus comes" (111). Among the figures Weber identifies as premillennialist, in addition to Robertson, are Jim Bakker, Oral Roberts, Rex Humbard, Jerry Falwell, Jimmy Swaggart and Richard DeHaan (216). Of these, one founded the Moral Majority; another stored up opulent treasures on earth, allegedly by misusing donations to his ministry, and one is, at this writing, seeking the Republican nomination for President of the United States. What sense can it make, if any, for these three men to be premillennialists? Do not their respective activities, ranging from the blatantly political to the absurdly materialistic, suggest a fundamental inconsistency between belief and practice?

This is, to be sure, a puzzling question. Weber, whom I would consider the leading authority on premillennialism, is mystified. Regarding Falwell, he says, "How does he put his premillennialism and his politics together? It is difficult to say, because Falwell does not make his eschatology explicit in his political views" (221). Joe Edward Barnhart, remarking on the waning of premillennialism among Southern Baptists, believes the issue became subsumed in the larger conflict over inerrancy, premillennialists and amillennialists cooperating with one another to battle non-inerrantists (56). What Barnhart calls "the postmillennial fantasy welling up again in premillennial hearts" is, he suggests, the result of anger, frustration, and a certain desire for revenge: "Even though the world cannot be saved, perhaps America can become a righteous nation, a Christian Israel on earth, where perverts can be put in their place and the Great Beast Liberalism mortally wounded" (165).

It is beyond the scope of this work to provide an in-depth analysis of fundamentalist political activism. Nor am I able to give a satisfactory "solution" to the contradiction between premillennialist theology and the rise of fundamentalist political activism.[13] Mindful of both Emerson and Foucault, I wonder too whether it is wise to insist on a "foolish consistency"; whether "contradictions are neither appearances to be overcome, nor secret principles to be uncovered" but "objects to be described for themselves" (*Archaeology* 151). I would, however, offer these observations for their inherent interest and potential for further analysis.

Where Weber saw premillennialists of the early twentieth century "shaken from their beliefs by the weariness of waiting" (51), we may be witnessing a similar phenomenon today. Fundamentalists also believe their very survival is threatened, fearing that their ability to continue their spiritual ministries is threatened by the bugbear of "secular humanism." In activist Tim LaHaye's words:

> If the atheistic, amoral, one-world humanists succeed in enslaving our country, that missionary outlet [i.e., America] will eventually be terminated. As a Christian and as a pastor, I am deeply concerned that this ministry be extended. The eternal souls of millions of people depend on us to supply them with the good news. In addition, I am concerned that the 50 million children who will grow up in America during the next generation will have access to the truth, rather than the heresies of humanism. (222–23)

I believe this passage reflects two important clues to the fundamentalist political phenomenon. On the one hand, fundamentalists justify their activism by claiming that it is necessary to maintaining their ability to "win souls."[14] More importantly, fundamentalists are deeply fearful for their children. When one considers their stock political concerns — abortion, homosexuality, school prayer, textbook censorship, pornography, the ERA — one sees a marked interest in those issues which directly concern the hearts and minds of children. Fundamentalists see a world where their own children are threatened by ungodly teaching in the public schools, where homosexuals lurk on playgrounds awaiting the chance to seduce the little ones with pornographic materials, where working mothers are so far from the domestic scene that children are left to their own pitiful devices. However alarmist or mistaken this view may be, one can appreciate that the perception of such a dire threat to one's own flesh and blood will motivate even the most diehard quietist to action.

Plain self-interest is at the root of political activism as well. LaHaye describes his entry into politics:

> I had never actively solicited candidates for political office. Then, in the providence of God, I was subjected to a painful educational experience, when the church attempted to get a zoning variance passed by the city council. After three years of effort, we lost, 6 to 2. For the first time, I realized that men and women largely hostile to the church controlled our city. (191)

That this episode should have been LaHaye's turning point from premillennialist quietism to activism reflects an almost laughable persecution complex, but his comments are echoed in explicitly premillennial terms by the pastor in *God's Choice*:

> It's too easy for us to get the idea that, well, the Lord is coming one of these days and we're on our way to heaven, and just forget about this whole world. Here's the way we finally began to think: We've got leaders that have caused our problems, and governments that have created difficulties for us in the operation of our ministries. So, as leaders we got together and said, "We've got to do something about this." (Peshkin 5)

It is one thing to describe the anxiety and arguably paranoiac worldview of fundamentalist leaders. But what is most intriguing is how successful these pastors have been in selling their premillennialist constituencies on activism so at variance with their tradition. In *God's Choice*, the pastor urges the women of his church to participate in an anti-ERA rally. "Some of you may think we're heading down a doubtful pass in doing this, but don't say this." He continues, "I'm not saying it's something you must do. I'm just making the opportunity available" (128). (Peshkin takes the pastor's sensitivity on this question to be a recognition of "the grayness of women's participation in politics" (128); I take it as the grayness of premillennialism.)

Jerry Falwell, on the other hand, has little patience with premillennialist misgivings: "Christians must keep America great by being willing to go into the halls of Congress, by getting laws passed that will protect the freedom and liberty of her citizens" (*Listen, America!* 227). For Falwell, political involvement is not optional:

Our ministry is as committed as it ever has been to the basic truths
of Scripture, to essential and fundamental Christian doctrines. But
we are not willing to isolate ourselves in seclusion while we sit back
and watch this nation plunge headlong toward hell. (225)

It comes as no surprise that every fundamentalist active in the political
milieu cites the Bible to defend his or her political beliefs. *Listen, America!*
and Tim LaHaye's *The Battle for the Mind,* to name just two fundamentalist manifestoes, constantly reference scripture in discussing issues of the
day. E.g., "A definite violation of holy Scripture, ERA defies the mandate
that 'the husband is the head of the wife, even as Christ is the head of
the church' (Ep. 5:23)" (*Listen, America!* 131). The authority of scripture
coupled with the authority of its expositor overcomes objections to the
futility or impropriety of political action. If the events of the last several
years tell us anything, it is that fundamentalist preachers wield immense
power over their flocks, mobilizing their departure from the church pew
into the voting booth. Seen in the light of premillennialist doctrine — an
often-overlooked aspect of fundamentalism — this power is all the more
striking.

Chapter 5

For Correction:
The Interpretive Community

*The only "proof" of membership is fellowship, the nod of
recognition from someone in the same community, someone who says to you what neither of us could ever prove
to a third party: "we know."*

Stanley Fish[1]

*But the natural man receiveth not the things of the Spirit
of God: for they are foolishness unto him: neither can he
know them, because they are spiritually discerned.*

1 Cor. 2.14

It has now become apparent that the Bible plays an integral role in
fundamentalism — not merely as an iconic object which a preacher thumps
and pounds, but as a bona fide text. It has also become apparent that in
order to comprehend fundamentalism, we must comprehend its distinctive
interpretation of the biblical text. We have seen that the inerrancy doctrine, held in common by all fundamentalists, and sub-species of that doctrine, literalism and dispensationalism, result in a particular interpretive
slant to the biblical text. When fundamentalists call our attention to the
plain teaching of the Word of God, when they claim that their own views
are merely paraphrases of the sacred text, we now have at least a sporting
chance of recognizing how their hermeneutics do indeed create textual
support for their views. One may question the validity of their interpretive
presuppositions, but not that of the resulting interpretations.

I now want to look at some specific examples of fundamentalist interpretations which stand in direct support of hermeneutical doctrines and
are, at one and the same time, consequences of doctrine. If the presump-
tion of textual inerrancy is a strategy for interpretation, it has certain consequences. Rather than simply reading the Bible, fundamentalists also
"write" that text. In Stanley Fish's words:

Interpretive communities are made up of those who share interpretive strategies not for reading (in the conventional sense) but for
writing texts, for constituting their properties and assigning their
intentions. In other words, these strategies exist prior to the act of
reading and therefore determine the shape of what is read rather
than, as is usually assumed, the other way around. (171)[2]

Fish's argument is indeed a controversial one: if he stops just short
of denying the existence of determinate meaning, he nevertheless implicitly
denies the possibility of finding that meaning. Like the famous tree falling
in the forest, texts are silent unless and until someone reads them. As the
following examples will demonstrate, however, fundamentalists do "write"
the Bible, particularly its problem passages, in accordance with interpretive
strategies which exist logically prior to the act of reading.

To illustrate these writing practices, I want to consider how the inerrancy doctrine has influenced some specific fundamentalist readings, past
and present. When Reuben A. Torrey wrote *Difficulties and Alleged Errors and Contradictions in the Bible* in 1907, he was less concerned with
factual and grammatical errors than with what might be called moral
difficulties — such troublesome narratives as the sacrifice of Isaac and the
slaughter of the Canaanites, for example. Torrey's explanations are often
disingenuous — "The Bible nowhere says that God commanded Abraham
to *slay* Isaac . . ." (39) — but they are for the most part concerned with
defending the morality of the Bible and its God than with niggling about
dates and numbers. But given the prodigious flowering of critical biblical
scholarship — evidence fundamentalists could no longer ignore in the hope
that it would just go away — Torrey's heirs have been forced to move
beyond the traditional worries of the Christian scholar — e.g., why did God
order the slaughter of Canaanite women and children? — into apparent
factual discrepancies. And move they do, often into their ultimate retreat —
the original autographs.[3]

Contemporary fundamentalist scholars are, by and large, quite willing
to chalk up obvious errors to the slip of a scribe's quill. Thus Archer
explains the dating discrepancy between 2 Kings 18.1 and 18.13 (71–72).
Scribal error is usually the fundamentalist's last resort, however; obviously,
it would be politically unwise to acknowledge more "errors" than absolutely
necessary in our existing biblical texts. Other mechanisms are brought
into play when possible. One of the most fascinating of these is the postulation of "gaps" in the biblical record.

The most famous gap is said to occur between Genesis 1.1 and 1.2.
Some fundamentalist scholars contend that Genesis 1.2 is more properly
translated "And the earth *became* without form, and void." With Genesis

1.2 then, the creation narrative of our own world begins. The gap is a large hole in the text, a pit into which one can dispose of such troublesome scientific evidence as the fossil record: "Relegate fossils to the primitive creation, and no conflict of science with the Genesis cosmogony remains" (*Scofield Reference Bible*, note to Gen. 1.11).[4] The ingenuity of this device aside, the gap theory illustrates a common practice of inerrantists — hypothesizing from what the text does *not* say. In *No Final Conflict*, Francis Schaeffer is somewhat troubled by the lack of "supporting verses" (26) for the Genesis gap theory and similar theories, but he defends what he calls "freedoms" (25) allowable to the interpreter in resolving textual difficulties. All of these freedoms involve creative interpolations in or extrapolations from the text, or more correctly what the text does not address. In short, as long as one does not contract the orthodox fundamentalist understanding of scripture, one is free to theorize however one wishes: in Schaeffer's words, "there is a certain possible range of freedom for discussion in the area of cosmogony while bowing to what God has affirmed" (36).

This technique can degenerate rather quickly into disregard for determining the actual facts of the case, effectively closing off discussion once the main objective — the protection of inerrancy — has been achieved. Lindsell reviews an Old Testament numerical discrepancy, the details of which are unimportant here, and concludes: "But whether one chooses [John] Calvin's or [Leon] Morris's solution, there is an answer to the problem that will satisfy anyone who is willing to look at it fairly" (168).

This stance — any answer will do, so long as it adheres to the inerrancy principle — is frequently found in fundamentalist scholarship. Sometimes the answers thus formulated are surprising. Lindsell, examining the differing Gospel accounts of Peter's denial of Christ, concludes that Peter denied Christ six times, rather than the traditional three (174–76). Matthew includes the Lord's Prayer as part of the Sermon on the Mount; in Luke's narrative, it appears while Jesus "was praying in a certain place" (Luke 11.1) after his visit with Martha and Mary. The *New Scofield* editors conclude that the Lord's Prayer "was evidently given upon two separate occasions" (note to Luke 11.2).[5] Both Scofield editions resolve the differing signs over the cross thusly:

> The narratives combined give the entire inscription: "This is [Matthew, Luke] Jesus [Matthew, John] of Nazareth [John] the King of the Jews [all]. (note to Matt. 27.37, brackets sic)

As one might expect, the fundamentalist is often faced with biblical material which seems contrary to fundamentalist religion. It is well known, for example, that most fundamentalists are teetotalers. How then do they justify the Cana miracle, where Jesus not only turns water into wine, but does so because the guests have drunk the host dry? Torrey, in a tour de force of literalistic interpretation, explains: "He provided wine, but there is not a hint that the wine He made was intoxicating. . . . New-made wine is never intoxicating" (96).

As these examples illustrate, the inerrancy doctrine generates a host of strained interpretations, many of which seem quite unnecessary to the preservation of Christian faith. Fundamentalists have a different priority: the preservation of the text, the preservation of their *doctrine* of the text. Particularly in the last two examples, one clearly perceives the interpretive tail wagging the textual dog. Scofield's artificial synthesis of the sign on the cross and Torrey's temperate wedding reception do not arise from the plain sense of the text but from a desperate need to stuff the Bible into an ill-fitting hermeneutical suit.[6]

These strained exegeses not only arise from interpretive strategies, but they are themselves evidence that these strategies exist logically prior to the text itself. If, as Foucault argues, discourses are "practices that systematically form the objects of which they speak," we might view these interpretations as the natural consequence of the inerrancy doctrine (*Archaeology* 49). Peculiar as they sometimes seem, the objects of which fundamentalists speak logically arise from their interpretive practices.

To make matters worse, every one of the fundamentalist interpretations I have cited thus far would be challenged by certain self-described fundamentalists, and every challenge would appeal to "what the Bible really says" on the matter. It is also vital to recognize that neither belief in biblical inerrancy nor literalistic Bible reading will, in and of themselves, assure that one turns out to be a Protestant fundamentalist. As our investigation of literalism demonstrated, reading scripture according to its plain sense does not generate unanimity of interpretation even among fundamentalists. Literal interpretation and application of certain scriptural passages are often deemed by fundamentalists themselves unnecessary or dangerous. Only a few denominations practice the sacrament of foot-washing, taking John 13.14 literally — "If I then, you Lord and Master, have washed your feet; ye also ought to wash one another's feet." Only a very few sects, fortunately, handle snakes and ingest poisons in literal obedience to Mark 16.18.

Indeed, the desire to read the scriptures unencumbered by tradition and *a priori* theological notions of what one *ought* to discover in the text has resulted in the formation of doctrines quite outside the pale of fundamentalism — and Christianity. As Nathan Hatch has noted, Unitarianism arose in just such fashion inasmuch as the doctrine of the Trinity is nowhere explicitly stated in the Bible (62–63). Robert K. Johnston observes that such heterodox sects as the Jehovah's Witnesses, The Way, and the Worldwide Church of God (founded by Herbert W. Armstrong) are inerrantist (10). Ultimately, the literalistic reader can reject Christianity in any form, concluding with H. L. Mencken that the plain sense of the scriptures reveals not a God deserving of worship but "the chartered libertine who is the hero of the Old Testament" (*Treatise on the Gods* 309).[7] The sole authority of the text can be a threat to the very order and authority that text is supposed to provide.

Because one's sense of what the text says arises from interpretive strategies that are in place before one applies those strategies to a problem passage, this state of affairs is a common one, one not restricted to fundamentalist interpretation. As Fish has noted, a literary critic, disputing the competing interpretation of an antagonist, frequently contends the antagonist "could not possibly be reading the same poem . . . and he would be right; for each of us would be reading the poem he had made" (169). Analyzing one such disagreement between two Blake critics (one of whom is E. D. Hirsch), Fish finds:

> What we have here then are two critics with opposing interpretations, each of whom claims the same word as internal and confirming evidence. Clearly they cannot both be right, but just as clearly there is no basis for deciding between them. One cannot appeal to the text, because the text has become an extension of the interpretive disagreement that divides them; and, in fact, the text as it is variously characterized is a *consequence* of the interpretation for which it is supposedly evidence. (340)

But Fish's contention here, although it is an apt characterization of what actually happens when readers interpret texts, is the sort of thing that will strike terror in the heart of the fundamentalist. When Fish acknowledges that there is no basis for adjudicating this dispute, he has just confirmed the fundamentalist's worst fear. On the one hand is the objective text maintaining order — on the other, epistemological chaos generating anarchy. B. B. Warfield, arguing against religious subjectivism, defines the options:

> Without such an "external authority" as a thoroughly trustworthy Bible, the soul is left without sure ground for a proper knowledge of itself, its condition, and its need, or for a proper knowledge of God's provisions of mercy for it and his promise of grace to it, —without sure ground, in a word, for its faith and hope. ("Inspiration" 70)

As one can readily see, the stakes in fundamentalist interpretation are high. This is no mere dispute about poetry; it concerns self-knowledge, one's purpose in this life and one's fate in the life beyond. And fundamentalists do not allow for privacy or pluralism in religious belief. At most, they may concede that non-fundamentalist Christians, however confused by "liberalism" or "popery," might nevertheless be admitted to heaven.

But is the fundamentalist's confidence sufficiently supported by the biblical text, or more precisely, *can* the Bible, even if it is "inerrant," provide the objective authority sought by fundamentalism? I here recall our earlier discussion of verbal inspiration. As Charles Hodge stated: "The thoughts are the words. The two are inseparable" (164). While there is much one can agree with in this proposition, Hodge himself illustrates its dubious utility when he remarks just seven pages later:

> The Bible was for ages understood and explained according to the Ptolemaic system of the universe; it is now explained without doing the least violence to its language, according to the Copernican system. (171)

Thus, while verbal inspiration would seem to rest on a rigid correspondence theory of language for it to have any practical value in interpretation, Hodge contends that the biblical writings on this subject can refer equally to two contradictory cosmogonies. Similarly, the contemporary scholar Clark Pinnock denies that new scientific discoveries undermine the "scripture principle": "Science has surely forced me to re-examine aspects of the traditional exegesis of the text, but it has by no means had the effect of discrediting the source or forcing me existentially to reinterpret it. Science has raised new questions for the text to answer but by no means has it replaced the Scriptures as the authority" ("How I Use the Bible" 32).

Pinnock explicitly contrasts the authority of the text with that of "traditional exegesis," and implicitly determines that the interpretations of his predecessors were mistaken. To use Hirsch's terminology, Pinnock appears to be distinguishing between the unchanging *meaning* of the text and the text's changing *significance*. One is hard pressed to discover, however, at what point *meaning* and *significance* become blurred. There is abundant evidence in the history of Christian exegesis that what we now recognize as significance was at one time considered beyond a shadow of a doubt to be meaning. The Roman church's treatment of Galileo is one prominent case in point. Hardly anyone nowadays accepts Ussher's chronology. Few fundamentalists now insist that the earth was created in six twenty-four hour days. Most fundamentalists, however, still insist that the theory of evolution contradicts the clear teaching of the Word of God; at present, they do not hesitate to proclaim evolution an ungodly theory. Only time will tell whether the familiar, disturbing pattern will repeat itself, whether fundamentalists eventually concede the validity of evolutionary theory, reinterpret relevant biblical passages, then carefully avoid recalling the acrimonious abuse once heaped by their predecessors on those who were right all along.

In actual practice, none of us hews very rigorously to Hirsch's careful distinction, in part because we are frequently unable to recognize the conditions under which a distinction is to be drawn. This state of affairs reflects badly on the soundness of Pinnock's argument as well as the validity of Hirsch's theory. To use fundamentalism as a test case of Hirsch demonstrates the extent to which his notion of determinate meaning can become exceedingly pernicious in the "wrong" hands. I would be very reluctant to say this danger is Hirsch's fault, however.[8] Although he has coined the term "cognitive atheist" to describe those who do not share his faith in objective interpretation (*Aims* 13), he would obviously not say that those who interpret Blake wrongly are putting their souls at risk if they persist in their error. Nor would he tell those of us who do not read Blake at all that we are thereby lacking knowledge vital to the salvation of our selves and our souls.

As a point of interest, however, Hirsch makes it quite plain that determinate meaning is, ultimately, an article of faith. In "The Politics of Theories of Interpretation," an article attacking such figures as Fish, Foucault, and Jacques Derrida as "idealists," Hirsch acknowledges that neither he nor his opponents can conclusively prove their respective positions. He then draws an analogy between his position and Pascal's wager:

> The modern version of Pascal's wager would be: Let us weigh the practical gain and loss in calling heads — that is, that objective historical truth exists. Let us estimate the two chances. If you win, you win something. If you lose, you lose nothing. Do not hesitate then, gamble on the existence of objective truth. (243)

He continues the analogy: "Thus, to be a realist or idealist in an ultimate epistemological sense is rather like being a theist or an atheist" (243). But Hirsch's analogy breaks down at a critical point, which is unfortunate for Hirsch but instructive for us. The whole point of Pascal's wager is lost unless the gamble is susceptible of ultimate verification. If you gamble on the truth of Christianity, you stand to win everything and lose nothing; if you gamble on its falsity, you stand to win nothing and lose everything. It is therefore difficult to appreciate how this wager could be legitimately applied to secular textual criticism; there is no possibility of finding out in the end whether one was right or wrong, unless Hirsch has postulated some literary-critical afterlife of which I'm unaware. Unless one has some means of verifying "the existence of objective truth," one can only assume its existence, an assumption that can rise no higher than the level of wishful thinking, which is not the sort of thinking that Hirsch, the champion of objective truth, generally recommends. By acknowledging that his own belief in determinate meaning is a wager, Hirsch acknowledges a fundamental indeterminacy at the heart of his own theory, and thereby fails to defend the high ground he has staked out against the "cognitive atheists." Hirsch's wager is thus of doubtful use to the perplexed literary critic, but because fundamentalists interpreters *do* posit an afterlife, Hirsch's wager and Pascal's wager are equally pertinent. Indeed, they are one and the same — it will make a difference, a momentous one, whether one properly apprehends the meaning of the Bible.

But is textual inerrancy necessary to that meaning? It is a doctrine that causes fundamentalists themselves no end of bother. Ever-vigilant, they must parry the assaults of "negative" and "destructive" critics, and must grapple with such mind-numbing matters as Old Testament genealogies and the reigns of Hebrew kings. But who are these critics? Only Beegle and Barr — Christians themselves — have made full frontal assaults on fundamentalist biblical interpretation; fundamentalist discourse is conspicuous only by its absence from mainstream religious journals. The critics cannot be those completely outside the fold; fundamentalist appeals to the authority of Christ and the self-testimony of the text will hardly make the desired impact on those who do not profess faith in the first place. Inerrancy anxiety is internal. The critics are primarily the alter egos of fundamentalists themselves, nagging voices inside their own heads. As Clark Pinnock has said, he "defended the strict view of inerrancy in my earlier years because I desperately wanted it to be true" (Frame, "Battle on the Bible" 44).[9]

But although Pinnock regards the Bible as "infallible" rather than "inerrant," his sense of scriptural authority is not markedly different from that of those who call themselves inerrantists.[10] In "How I Use the Bible in Doing Theology," he says, "Adherence to the Bible for me means acquiescence to all its teachings and a refusal to allow any rival to stand above it, whether tradition, reason, culture, science, or opinion" (19). He believes, in short, that Christianity must "[locate] the basis of authority in the objective written Word of God." (19). He criticizes those theologians who do not support "biblical infallibility," including those who claim that because "the Scriptures still have to be interpreted by fallible persons" authority cannot be grounded in an infallible text even if such a text existed (21).

Pinnock evinces a rather more subtle understanding of interpretation than one often finds among conservatives. He acknowledges, for example, that all Bible readers approach the text with presuppositions: "One's pre-understanding of the Bible either as God's infallible Word or as merely human traditions from which both illuminating and distorting ideas come is critical to one's use of the Bible" (21–22). [11] It is by no means easy to determine what the Bible "says" (23–24), but for Pinnock, the answer does not lie in breaking the ground rules of one's interpretive community, and here Pinnock would mean Christianity itself, wondering "just how scholarship which does *not* assume coherence in the Scriptures can credibly be called Christian scholarship" (25). Hirsch's wager is echoed: "Perfect objectivity is not something we can achieve, but it is an ideal we can strive for by consciously opening ourselves to criticism and correction both by God, speaking through the text, and by the convictions of others" (31). That is, one must seek the authorial consciousness, present in the text, and one must also be open to the contributions of fellow members of one's interpretive community.[12] One cannot "pick and choose" among Bible doctrines, Pinnock warns; one must endeavor to interpret "each text in the canonical context," being convicted as an article of faith that "everything in Scripture is meant to be there and to have value" (25–26). Pinnock is quite aware that interpretation occurs within the context of a particular community or tradition. "The biblical faith is never found apart from tradition. It does not exist in pure essence free of historical forms and fallibilities. But the essence and the forms are not identical and must not be equated" (34). Traditions must be, Pinnock concludes, ever susceptible to the "biblical message" (34).

But even in Pinnock's comparatively moderate analysis, is not the biblical text still, in Fish's words, "a consequence of the interpretation for which it is supposedly evidence"? Despite Pinnock's own recognition that interpreters always, inevitably play a role in adducing textual meaning, he nevertheless asserts the discrete existence of a "biblical message" which in some unexplained way must stand in judgment of all interpretive comers.

The Bible is no exception to the fact that any text serves as the court of appeal for interpretations arising therefrom. Whether believer or non-believer in determinate meaning, anyone who appeals to the text to validate his or her interpretation of it is making the claim that the text says *this* rather than *that*. On one level, it makes no difference whether the formulation is "Blake says" or "God says." But Blake, of course, is not God — and what we commonly hear from fundamentalists is that they alone apprehend the true, objective, absolute, determinate meaning of the Bible. The corollaries are obvious: their interpretations, alone, are correct and finally, according to the more extreme fundamentalists, they alone possess saving truth. As John R. Rice puts it:

I know the use of the English language, and one is either ignorant or avoiding the plain intent of language when he accuses me or other fundamentalists of being mean and narrowminded in using Bible language to mean what the Bible means and to use dictionary definitions for facts that are openly apparent and acknowledged by all. (171)

Rice's strategy here is a common one. Stanley Fish, remarking on its use by literary critics, characterizes the strategy as "a move drenched in humility, although it is often performed with righteousness: those other fellows may be interested in displaying their ingenuity, but *I* am simply a servant of the text" (353).[13] You may think you are disputing me, Rice implies, but really you are disputing God, whose Word I faithfully and humbly expound. Although one would instinctively resist putting Rice and the moderate J.I. Packer in the same class, consider what Packer has to say about his participation in the 1986 summit of the International Council on Biblical Inerrancy: "The three hundred of us who met at the Summit believe that anyone who allows Scripture to deliver its own message on these matters will end up approximately where we stand ourselves" (Frame, "Inerrancy Council" 39).

In his article, "In Quest of Canonical Interpretation," Packer covers most of the usual terrain: tradition is important but ultimately subordinate to the Bible itself; the message of the Bible is "coherent and self-consistent" (49); "certainties must be distinguished from possibilities" (an echo of Schaeffer's "freedoms") (52). But what is most interesting is Packer's introduction, where he makes a great point of stressing that the article is a personal statement, expressing revulsion at the thought he might attract "disciples" (36). Why should he be worried about this?

Because anyone who voices certainties as a Christian in directly personal terms runs the risk of being misheard, as if to be saying: "Believe this, or do that, because it is what I believe and do, and my own experience has proven that it is right;" in other words, "take it from *me,* as if I were your God and authority." (36)

I would not doubt the sincerity of Packer's remarks, nor would I fail to commend him for recognizing a danger too often either ignored or willfully exploited by his cohorts. Yet whatever the decency of Packer's motives here, his strategy simply does not work. The fundamentalist tendency to view its "certainties" as universally valid assures that anyone who disagrees with key tenets of fundamentalist doctrine will usually be accused of disagreeing with God.

As Packer correctly observes in *"Fundamentalism" and the Word of God,* doctrinal disputes arise when there is lack of consensus on authority:

> The deepest cleavages in Christendom are doctrinal; and the deepest doctrinal cleavages are those which result from disagreement about authority. Radical divergences are only to be expected when there is no agreement as to the proper grounds for believing anything. (44)

One must give due credit to Packer's judgment here, for he is entirely correct in discerning that doctrine is authority in verbalized form. His statement cuts across all disciplinary boundaries; I would not be writing this book today had I stated in my graduate school application that Shakespeare was a ninth-rate hack. The medical student who believes malignant tumors are better prayed than cut away will likely be drummed out of the profession before she ever enters an operating room. Likewise, had I truly loathed Shakespeare, or had my hypothetical medical student been a devotee of divine healing, it is likely that neither of us would have applied to our respective institutions in the first place. Why would we, when we disagree with the fundamental doctrines of those institutions?

But Packer immediately follows the useful statement above by making a problematic distinction between two classes of doctrinal disputes. On the one hand are such clashes as those between Calvinists and Arminians: "both sides agreed that Scripture is the final authority and differed only as to what it teaches" (44). The second category, exemplified by the conflict between Protestantism and Roman Catholicism, is characterized by disagreement over the locus of authority. Is the text the only authority, or does authority arise from both the text and the interpretive institution?

I would argue that Packer's distinction is viable only superficially; of what possible use is a supremely authoritative text when interpreters cannot then agree on what the text says or "teaches"? Quibbles over eschatology are a prime case in point. Although the options available to "Bible believers" are dizzying in their variety and hardly self-evident in the biblical text, eschatology is an extremely divisive issue. Timothy Weber remarks:

> Even though the differences seem insignificant to outsiders, many premillennialists refuse to appear on the same platforms, serve on the same theological faculties, or be in the same churches with fellow premillennialists who hold, for example, a different view of the timing of the rapture. In such cases, the people involved believe that biblical truth, even orthodoxy is at stake. (240–41)

Not all fundamentalists are quite so precise. *Christianity Today,* in its recent symposium, "Our Future Hope: Eschatology and Its Role in the Church," allows that individuals with good evangelical credentials might legitimately disagree even on the particulars of the millennium itself. Nevertheless, Gleason Archer, one symposium participant, would make it a test for church leadership: "If a person approaches Scripture from a different point of view than the rest of the church, he is not ready for church leadership" (9–I).

Note that for Archer the issue ultimately devolves to how one reads scripture, not the exact position one takes on the eschatological issues in question. Although Archer says that this "is an area in which evangelical Christians may disagreee," he is emphatic in declaring that it ought not to be considered a "secondary" issue (4–I). And it is another participant on the panel, John Walvoord, who makes it absolutely plain why this is so: "Generally speaking, most premillennialists are also strong proponents of inerrancy. Now, with all deference to Dr. Hoekema [Anthony Hoekema, an amillennialist evangelical], if a person is amillennial, you really don't know a thing about his view of Scripture because he's denied the millennium" (4–I). Hoekema responds by saying, in effect, that he *does* believe in the millennium, explaining that he does not "take literally" what premillennialists have chosen to take literally, and pointedly noting that premillennialists do not "take everything literally, either" (5–I). Thus even the most apparently trivial issue becomes directly related to one's adherence to the inerrancy doctrine and literalistic interpretation.

After spending some three hundred pages of *God, Revelation and Authority* on inerrancy, many of which are spent attacking James Barr, Carl F. H. Henry then warns against "unbalanced preoccupation" with the doctrine, regarding such preoccupation as a hindrance to doing productive theology and as tending toward exclusivism.[14] He may well have a point, but could the situation be otherwise, given that an inerrant Scripture is the very ground of fundamentalism?

Fundamentalists are caught in the very trap they try to avoid. They must resort to some form of institutional authority, unless they want to grant authority to the interpretations of any reader whatsoever who espouses the inerrancy doctrine. The ultimate difficulty with textual inerrancy is that it necessarily requires an inerrant reader. While Packer tries to sidestep the Calvinist-Arminian controversy and Machen minimizes the post/premillennialist conflict, neither can overcome the compelling logic of inerrant readership. Try as they might to be humble, to avoid the pitfalls of intellectual pride — largely because the Bible tells them to, perhaps — fundamentalists are dogmatic and doctrinalistic because their doctrine of the text forces them to be. They are reading an inerrant text; what they read, and therefore by definition what they *interpret*, must be inerrant.

We are now at a difficult crossroads, one which many fundamentalists do not even recognize. The sole authority of the text is subverted by the very nature of texts. How does the fundamentalist control interpretation, while claiming at the same time that nothing but the text itself is authoritative?

The controls are many, as we shall see in the next chapter. But among the leaders of fundamentalism, one begins to perceive what Fish calls the "nod of recognition," a fraternal sensibility palpable to members of the club, mystifying to those who do not belong. Outsiders are "natural men" who "receive not the things of God." Their comments and criticisms are summarily dismissed at best, viciously condemned at worst.[15] Dewey Beegle, for example, has been characterized by Harold Lindsell as "incapable of clear thinking" (171). Gleason Archer finds "no great difference" between Beegle's attitude toward the Bible and that of the nineteenth-century polemicist Robert Ingersoll (76), an agnostic and vocal critic of Christianity. Because he attacks the inerrancy doctrine, Beegle, a Christian scholar and a relatively conservative one at that, is compared to a notorious infidel.

But if one's attitude is right, one can even espouse errancy and inerrancy at the same time, as Arthur Carl Piepkorn reveals in his fascinating article, "What Does 'Inerrancy' Mean?" Although he concludes that *inerrancy* is not a useful term, citing most of the problems I have already discussed, he warns, for "pastoral reasons" against disavowing it (593). In other words, the authority of the discourse would be threatened if pastors let on to the person in the pew that the scriptures are not without error after all. Piepkorn further advises that one just stop using the term, without elaboration; if pressed on one's views, one is not encouraged to lie, but one should certainly refuse to be badgered into a yes-or-no response. While Piepkorn would undoubtedly be taken to task by some fundamentalists, the more moderate among them would find no cause to fault his attitude toward either the Bible or the authority of the discourse.

One's attitude, in short, counts for a great deal. *Attitude* is not easily defined, but fundamentalists make recurring appeals to it when confronted with individuals whose discourse threatens the authority of fundamentalist discourse. Thus far, I have said almost nothing about *faith*, an ingredient usually found in religions, because fundamentalism itself so thoroughly emphasizes the virtues of rationality and objectivity. When apologists are backed into a corner, however, they do appeal to faith, the connotation of which is far better understood as a political attitude rather than as a spiritual condition.

In *The Battle for the Bible,* Lindsell contends that non-inerrantists are, finally, just perverse and impious: "May not the real difficulty be a want of biblical faith rather than a want of evidence?" (161). Similarly, Reuben A. Torrey argues that dwelling on textual difficulties and defects "reveals a great perversity of both mind and heart" (14). The influence of Scottish Common Sense philosophy on fundamentalist thought, a subject helpfully explored by historian George Marsden, may help to account for such remarks. Because Common Sense epistemology asserts that "basic truths are much the same for all persons in all times and places" (Marsden 111), its adherents are virtually incapable of accounting for honest disagreement among interpreters (114–16). "Among traditional explanations were moral error, faulty reasoning, speculative hypotheses, metaphysical fancies and the prejudices of unbelief or false religions" (116).

If inerrancy is, as its defenders contend, as plain as the nose on one's face, it would indeed follow that its discreditors are willfully perverse. But it is ironic that Lindsell is required to make an appeal to one's subjective apprehension of God in order to substantiate his objectivist reading of scripture. Mark A. Noll, an evangelical scholar, is much less alarmed than Lindsell by creeping errancy in fundamentalist circles, yet he too seeks to discern among good and bad attitudes toward the Bible, claiming that some interpretive models carry negative "presuppositions" about biblical errancy, and do not therefore approach the text with a sufficiently high regard for its authority (112–115). The fundamentalist scholar J. Barton Payne carries this argument further, implying that the very exercise of critical judgment will lead inexorably to bias and impiety:

> But once theory moves away from description into evaluation and begins to adopt a negative stance toward the data it is supposed to be explaining . . . at that moment it has gone beyond its tether and placed itself in opposition to the standards of Jesus. (96)

Although the standards of Jesus here have to do only with Jesus's "teaching" on the inerrancy of scripture, the charge of disobedience against God is unmistakable.

The standards of Jesus notwithstanding, moral findings against interpreters with whom one disagrees are the logical result of belief in determinate meaning, a belief Payne must hold if he believes it is possible for one to describe and explain textual "data" without evaluating it. As Stanley Fish has remarked: "To someone who believes in determinate meaning, disagreement can only be a theological error. The truth lies plainly in view, available to anyone who has the eyes to see; but some readers choose not to see it and perversely substitute their own meanings for the meanings that texts obviously bear" (338). By understanding how belief in determinate meaning will affect one's response to antagonists, we can appreciate why fundamentalists attack their critics with such moralistic vigor.

Our analysis of fundamentalist biblical interpretation — from the doctrine of biblical inerrancy through its tendency towards literalism to the function of the interpretive community — has brought us to a rather odd pass. We have seen that the Bible does indeed do what fundamentalists claim it does: it functions as their sole authority. We have also seen that the inherence of interpretation prevents *any* text from functioning as such an authority.

While these issues have long been the focus of contemporary literary-critical argument, anxiety, and animosity, most fundamentalists show little awareness that these issues are admissible or even relevant to their work. We need not chalk this failure up to intellectual bankruptcy; men like Pinnock, Packer, and the late Francis Schaeffer are by no means intellectually ill-equipped. We need only recognize that it would be literally impossible for any fundamentalist to credit the theories of a Fish or a Foucault, for in so doing, the fundamentalist would cease to be a fundamentalist.

As we now turn to examination of the roles of extra-textual authorities, we will need to bear in mind two important points. There can be no authority without the contributions of extra-textual agents. But in order for those agents to be effective, they must necessarily deny their existence, subsuming their work in the sole authority of the Word of God. Because the sole authority of the Word is the proclaimed hallmark of fundamentalist discourse, those individuals in positions of authority may not even be fully aware themselves of the role they play in constituting authority. Their denials may well be unconscious and uncontrived, for the "rules that characterize a discursive practice. . .are not imposed from the outside on the elements that they relate together; they are caught up in the very things that they connect" (Foucault, *Archaeology* 127).

Chapter 6

For Instruction in Righteousness: The Authority of Interpreters

What Scripture says, God says; and what God says in Scripture is to be the rule of faith and life in His Church.

J.I. Packer[1]

Obey them that have the rule over you, and submit yourselves; for they watch for your souls, as they that must give account, that they may do it with joy, and not with grief: for that is unprofitable for you.

Hebrews 13.17

God never intended for the committee nor a board of deacons nor any other group to dominate a church or control a pastor. The pastor is God's man, God's servant, God's leader.

Jerry Falwell[2]

We have now seen in some detail that the fundamentalist doctrines of the Bible are problematical. Both the definition and application of hermeneutical principles raise numerous problems, ranging from logical difficulties inherent in the principles themselves to strained exegesis of specific problem passages and inconsistencies in interpretation among interpreters who all agree on the basic rules. Fundamentalist anxiety about the locus of authority can only be aggravated by disagreements among interpreters; such disagreements, I have argued, demonstrate that the inerrant text, even if it does exist, has little practical value unless it is read by inerrant interpreters.

Although a thorough examination of the difficulties inherent in fundamentalist interpretation of the text has been a necessary part of our analysis of fundamentalist authority, we must also bear in mind that fundamentalists themselves would either disbelieve the analysis or for various reasons find it irrelevant. Many, in fact, are truly unaware that inerrancy, literalism or dispensationalism are in any way untenable approaches to the biblical text. As we shall see, fundamentalist authorities go to great lengths to keep the rank-and-file unsullied by subversive material. One cannot adequately appreciate the power of extra-textual authorities, such as preachers or commentators, without recognizing that the interpretive presuppositions upon which their pronouncements are based are largely invisible to the person in the pew. Such persons have little basis for disputing statements and arguments which appear to be found in the Bible "itself." If we can empathize with lay fundamentalists, if we can share for the moment their belief that the Bible is the inerrant, verbally inspired word of God, we shall find it relatively easy to comprehend the power of extra-textual authorities.

These authorities are both internal and external to the reader. All readers are to pray for guidance in interpreting the scripture and to accept the leading of the Holy Spirit in answer to such prayers: "The Scriptures are to be interpreted under the guidance of the Holy Spirit, which guidance is to be humbly and earnestly sought" (Hodge 187). External authority rests in accredited interpreters and commentators; one gains accreditation by adhering to fundamentalist hermeneutics, and usually too by being one of "them that have the rule over" the laity , whether as pastor, Bible college instructor, or author of commentary. And the more highly a text is valued, the more commentary proliferates; in Foucault's words,

> the top-heaviness of the original text, its permanence, its status as discourse ever capable of being brought up to date, the multiple or hidden meanings with which it is credited, the reticence and wealth it is believed to contain, all this creates an open possibility for discussion. (*Discourse* 221)

Yet it is also the role of commentary to patrol the boundaries of discourse, ensuring that fidelity to the original text is maintained. Foucault continues:

> Commentary averts the chance element of discourse by giving it its due: it gives us the opportunity to say something other than the text itself, but on condition that it is the text itself which is uttered and, in some ways, finalised. (221)

It is this duality — the utterance together with the finalization of a text — that I want to explore in this chapter. I am proposing that fundamentalism has succeeded marvelously in covering its *finalization* of the text with the cloak of *utterance*. By denying that authority arises in community, to use Fish's term, or in discourse, to use Foucault's, the door may well be open for a tyranny of interpretation, in which authoritative interpreters are able to exercise power over their subjects by effacing the distinction between text and interpretation, an effacement especially apparent in literalistic reading when it is claimed that the interpreter does nothing more than expound the "plain sense" of the text. Even when interpreters explictly disclaim infallibility, the disclaimer is usually accompanied by a strong doctrinal statement sufficient to ensure that the interpreter's remarks will nevertheless be taken very seriously indeed. In the introduction to the *Liberty Commentary on the New Testament*, Jerry Falwell writes: "Our interpreters do not claim infallibility, but each one is a born-again Bible believer who accepts the inerrant inspiration of the Scripture and believes the Bible to be the only message of eternal life" (iii). Thus the interpreters establish their credentials, and ally themselves with the absolute text. It is important to note, however, that Falwell's statement cuts both ways. Interpreters are not free to say whatever they want; they are bound by the rules of their discourse, the authority of which exists independently of any given individual. Edward Said's remarks apropros of literary criticism are equally applicable here:

> You have to pass through certain rules of accreditation, you must learn the rules, you must speak the language, you must master the idioms, and you must accept the authorities of the field — determined in many of the same ways — to which you want to contribute. ("Opponents, Audiences" 8)

In direct consequence of their fidelity to these rules of accreditation, interpreters possess considerable control over the reading and thus the beliefs of the common believer. The question this chapter poses is this — at what point do the interpretations of pious, Bible believing men and (rarely) women approach the canonicity of scripture itself?

The influence and authority of written commentary are best understood through examining the status of the *Scofield* and *New Scofield* reference Bibles in fundamentalist circles. Critics of fundamentalism generally agree that the Scofield commentary becomes for many readers tantamount to scripture itself. Beegle says:

> The influence of the Scofield notes became so dominant within evangelical circles that many adherents considered the commentary as *the true interpretation* of the Bible, thus implicitly granting the commentary equal authority with the biblical text. The average reader did not have enough training or insight to see that in many instances the distinctive features of dispensationalism represented only one or two or more alternative explanations of the text. (110)

The commentaries are influential, gaining a certain prestige simply because of their proximity to the biblical text and their inclusion within a book whose cover says "The Holy Bible." As Frank Kermode reminds us, "We should never underestimate our predisposition to believe what is presented under the guise of an authoritative report and is also consistent with the mythological structure of a society from which we derive comfort, and which it may be uncomfortable to dispute" (*Genesis* 113).

We have already examined the original *Scofield Reference Bible*, edited by Scofield himself, in our discussion of dispensationalism. The *New Scofield* was published in 1967, well after Scofield's death, by a committee of commentators. It is distinguished not only by its dispensationalism, but by a marked increase in commentary. While Scofield confined himself primarily to dispensationalism per se, his successors have made major changes in the content and scope of the original edition. A comparison of the two editions reveals some fascinating editorial choices. The *New Scofield* is not nearly so blatant in diminishing the authority of the Gospels, although it remains the case that the dispensation of grace begins after the death of Christ. This renewed attention to the Gospels is required by the new editors' emphasis on the authority of Christ as an expositor of biblical inerrancy. E.g., "Christians should follow their Lord in taking these five books as actually the work of this great prophet" (note to Ex. 17.14). The implicit appeal here to the piety of the reader — one is actively disobeying Christ if one questions Moses's authorship of the entire Pentateuch — is a recurrent theme in the new notes. The editors in effect suggest that to question the inerrancy of the gospels is to reveal that one is not Christian at all:

> The important thing to keep in mind is the established fact that these Gospels are inspired historical documents of genuine authenticity and full integrity. Moreover, the believer in Christ knows in his own life the reality of the living Lord, who is so faithfully and yet so variously presented in the Synoptics and in John's Gospel. (from the preface to "The Four Gospels")

This is an interesting twist on personal experience, so often downgraded by fundamentalists. If one cannot recognize the authenticity of the Gospels, the argument goes, it is because one has never had a personal encounter with Christ, without which of course one cannot be saved. To the extent that the salvation experience is placed in the service of the text, however, we see once again an indication that one's personal experience of Christ is subordinated to the authority of the biblical text. An individual claiming that his or her impression of Christ differs from the manner in which Christ is portrayed in the Gospels will be told in no uncertain terms that his or her experience is, therefore, false.

The King James Version is still the translation used, but the *New Scofield* editors take interesting liberties with certain passages. Archaic words are remanded to the margins, because "language is not static" (Introduction v). The editors sanitize "indelicate words or expressions" (vi), and my cursory check of possible indelicacies reveals that the dung and piss of 2 Kings 18.27 have been refined into refuse and water; "him that pisseth against the wall" in 1 Kings 14.10 is now less graphically "every male."

While Scofield was much given to typology, he did not generally use his notes to draw moral lessons from biblical narratives. His successors do so freely and often rather harshly: "One thief was saved, so that none needs to despair; but only one, so that none may presume" (note to Luke 23.43). Scofield said the imprecatory Psalms were "a cry unsuited to the church" (Preface to the Psalms). The *New Scofield* not only deletes this remark; it notes at Ps. 109.1 that such cries are quite suited to the church indeed. While stating that some believers acknowledge the "progressiveness of revelation," the weight of the comment is definitely on the side of calling down divine vengeance:

> The righteous indignation of those who love God is justifiable against injustice, malevolence, lawlessness, and especially against apathy toward or rebellion against Him. God's servants await the day when righteousness will be rewarded and unrighteousness will be punished....

Given the popularity of the Scofield notes, it is crucial to recognize the markedly strident tone of the new edition; overall, this edition is far more militant than the original. Most noteworthy is the increase in amount of notes, reflecting the desire to control more closely the interpretations of the ordinary reader.

It is ironic that commentary has become so influential in a movement purportedly devoted to the sole authority of the text. As Weber remarks, "Despite the claims that lay people could study the Bible for themselves, their teachers rarely let them" ("Two-Edged Sword" 113). Weber uses the Scofield Bible as a specific case in point. The perspicuity of scripture is belied by numerous dispensational novelties, especially the conclusion that the Lord's Prayer is not appropriate to the present age, something the ordinary reader, untutored by commentary, would almost certainly fail to discern (114). "In the final analysis," Weber concludes, "there is something incongruous about fundamentalists who say that they can read the Bible by themselves, then pore over Scofield's notes in order to discover what the text really means" (114).[3] While it must be remembered that not all fundamentalists are dispensationalists, the influence of the Scofield commentary illustrates one means by which extra-textual authorities have successfully controlled the interpretations of the ordinary reader.[4]

We must also determine, in Foucault's words, who is "accorded the right" to speak. From what "institutional *sites*" do they speak? (*Archaeology* 50-51). Our determination here must be made with the recognition that discursive rules "operate not only in the mind or consciousness of individuals, but in discourse itself; they operate therefore, according to a sort of uniform anonymity, on all individuals who undertake to speak in this discursive field" (63). To gain a hearing, therefore, one must obey the rules of one's discourse.

In every fundamentalist setting, there is a preoccupation with the "soundness" of secondary sources, whether persons or texts, and a corresponding proscription of that which in any way threatens fundamentalist authority. Barr explains how soundness is defined:

> Just as there is one book, the Bible, which is in all respects infallible and inerrant, so there are, on a secondary level, books that are 'sound' and wholesome because they *say* that the Bible is infallible and inerrant, and attack the critics who cast doubt upon this. (121)

Daniel Stevick, in his insightful *Beyond Fundamentalism*, observes that soundness is the primary criterion for judging any extra-textual authority:[5]

> The first question about an unknown speaker, book or organization is: "Is he (or it) 'sound'? Does he conform to our pattern of theological statement." ... I have often heard among Fundamentalists certain theologians solemnly appraised as "All right, but 'off' on the second coming." (52)

It is crucial, of course, that teachers, and outside speakers in fundamentalist educational institutions be sound, given their strong influence on the intellectual development of students. Fundamentalists in the Southern Baptist Convention, waging a "holy war" for control of their denomination, recognize that gaining that control will depend on gaining control of the denomination's seminaries. In an interview with Joe Edward Barnhart, Harold Lindsell advocates the removal of faculty members who do not believe "that Adam and Eve were historical figures, Moses wrote the Pentateuch, and the Book of Isaiah has only one author." He adds, "I'm on the board of trustees for Gordon-Conwell Theological Seminary in Massachusetts. I can tell you now, we'd remove from our faculty anyone who uses redaction criticism on the Bible or anyone who didn't believe in biblical inerrancy" (5).

As Stevick also points out, soundness goes beyond mere fidelity to fundamentalist biblical hermeneutics into fluency with communal linguistic formulations, leading to what Stevick perceptively calls "justification by correct statement" (53):

> A way of talking, a way of acting, a body of predictable responses, have grown up within Fundamentalism, and conformity with these is the criterion of acceptance.... A quite specific group of catchphrases mark (sic) a Fundamentalist. Some of them, such as "infallible Word," "second coming," "Jesus saves," "accepting Christ," and "personal savior," are not strictly biblical. Yet these shibboleths are made the basis for inclusion or exclusion by a group which claims sole and supreme loyalty to the Bible. (56)

Barnhart notes this habit too, observing that fundamentalists "use the phrase 'the blood of Christ' frequently and ritualistically in their sermons and are suspicious of ministers who do not" (70). Peshkin's *God's Choice* is a valuable source of fundamentalist cliches, always apparent in the speech of both teachers and students. Those students who are "backslidden" and not "living for the Lord," to use a few such cliches myself, find that their language gives them away; one such student says of a teacher: "Because we had written a composition about something, and she didn't like what we had wrote (sic), she said, 'I can tell by this composition that you are not saved' "(245).

The use of jargon and cliches to signify one's membership in a particular community is not a phenomenon restricted to fundamentalism, but it does indicate the extent to which the fundamentalist's use of both biblical language — what Barr calls the "incantational use of scripture" (37) — and extra-biblical idioms is a means of establishing a speaker's orthodoxy. The person who says simply, "I believe in Jesus Christ" is far less likely to establish his or her fundamentalist credentials than the individual who attests, "I have accepted Jesus Christ as my personal Lord and Savior."

The care taken to shield fundamentalist laypersons from non-fundamentalist discourse reflects the strong belief that the wrong words, the wrong combination of words, can subvert faith — an attitude traceable to the centrality of an inerrant text, without which fundamentalists claim that faith itself can be destroyed. It is not surprising that fundamentalist institutions exercise careful control over the secondary reading material of the laity. Joe T. Olde, a Southern Baptist conservative, opposes the inclusion of "Biblical criticism" in Southern Baptist curricular materials, and in so doing exposes his fear that the laity, unlike the clergy, are unable to cope with it: "No one will deny that Biblical criticism, when carefully and wisely used, has a proper place, but many would question whether that place is in quarterlies used by the rank and file of Southern Baptists" (Barnhart 34).[6]

There are only two places for a Bultmann or a Tillich volume — in a classroom where a qualified authority can declare these thinkers "wrong," or the bonfire. And there is a corresponding interest in seeing that the layperson be exposed as much as possible to sound teaching. One sees rigid *government* of the individual in Foucault's sense of that term — "To govern, in this sense, is to structure the possible field of action of others" ("The Subject and Power" 221). In addition to Sunday School and Sunday morning worship service, fundamentalist churches hold Sunday evening services and a mid-week Bible study and prayer meeting. The larger the church the fuller the schedule can become. As Frances Fitzgerald has reported, the various functions at Thomas Road Baptist Church — Jerry Falwell's church — are so numerous that one "could spend all his or her time in church or in church-related activities. In fact, many church members do just that" (73). The now-notorious former church secretary Jessica Hahn describes her life prior to her fateful encounter with Jim Bakker: "church *was* my whole life. Friday night was church; Saturday night was choir practice; Sunday night was church; Tuesday morning was church; Wednesday morning was church..."(85).

Keeping so busy with church activities that one has little time for anything else is, in part, the practical outworking of a doctrine espoused by the more extreme fundamentalists — that of *separation*, for which the primary supporting Bible verse is 2 Cor. 6.14: "Be ye not unequally yoked together with unbelievers: for what fellowship hath righteousness with unrighteousness? and what communion hath light with darkness?" Separation means, for example, that fundamentalists ought not to cooperate with other Christians who are not fundamentalist; as John R. Rice makes clear, such Christians are in fact not Christians at all:

> We are clearly against calling infidels Christians, having them join our churches, teaching in our Sunday schools or seminaries, or leading in prayer in revival campaigns, or serving on committees in denominations or revivals, as if they were Christians. An infidel is not a Christian. The two ought not to be treated alike according to the plain Scriptures. (155)

(Rice defines *infidel* to include those who deny the virgin birth and the bodily resurrection of Jesus [171].)

Second Corinthians 6.14 is also taken to encompass the entire spectrum of human relationships — marriage, friendship, social affiliations and business associations. The church pastor in Peshkin's *God's Choice* says:

> We're not to be in partnership or relationship with the untruthful works of darkness. We are to reprove them or we are to convict them. One way the Bible teaches us to convict them is by not having any fellowship with them. (9)

By insulating themselves from the world — being in the world and not of it, to use the biblical language — strict fundamentalists develop a deep distrust of non-fundamentalists. A teacher describes her feelings to Peshkin:

> I can't have confidence in a person if he's not saved. I have no right to expect anything, really, from them. I can't expect real understanding, because they don't know the God of understanding. I can't expect true compassion and love, even though they are very, very good people. (271)

A key figure in creating and maintaining these controls is the church pastor — part administrator and part biblical expositor. In the "chain of command" — a popular fundamentalist philosophy of order applied to church, family, and secular government — the pastor is the spiritual leader of his flock, and the sheep are to "submit" to their shepherd, in the same way that wives are to submit to their husbands (Eph. 5.22) and citizens to their governments (Rom 13.1).[7] Peshkin provides abundant evidence of the close control exercised over both students and teachers in the fundamentalist Christian school. The rules are many and strict; the virtues of obedience and submission to authority within the chain of command are emphasized not only to students but to teachers and church members are well. E.g., "Guided by scriptural injunctions about authority, we [teachers] are to be submissive to our administrators" (82).

While the polity of most churches identifying themselves as evangelical is reasonably democratic, the government of self-described fundamentalist churches resembles nothing so much as an elected dictatorship. As example, we can consider the philosophy of church government held by America's most notorious local church pastor, Jerry Falwell, pastor of the Thomas Road Baptist Church in Lynchburg, Virginia. *Church Aflame*, a book cowritten by Falwell and Elmer Towns, states: "There is no court of appeal beyond the pastor. . . . If a pastor abuses this authority, then the congregation has the right to remove the pastor"(188).[8] Falwell is adamant that all persons in positions of leadership in the church be in total submission to the chief pastor: "The Christian education program of the church begins with the pastor, not the minister of Christian education nor the youth director" (51). Sunday School teachers sign a "covenant" in which they pledge to "teach from the Word of God, using the lessons approved by the Pastor and Education Director" and to "be loyal to the Pastor and program of the Thomas Road Baptist Church" (107-08). According to Falwell, effective church governance is impossible unless it is under the control of one man — "God's man." "You can't have ten men running a business or ten people running a church" (183).

John R. Rice cites the seventh and seventeenth verses of Hebrews 13 in support of his belief in the sole authority of the church pastor. Although pastors are well advised to "seek the counsel of others," Rice makes it quite clear that those others have no real power:

> The deacons are never mentioned as having any rule over the churches, and it is a modern idea to have a board of deacons decide matters for the church. That is not taught in the Bible. The word *deacon* means servant, and so the deacons are the servants of the church and should work under the direction of the pastor.... Since pastors are human and have the same human frailty that everybody else has, they will sometimes make mistakes. But usually the pastor is more likely to know the will of God than others, if he is God's man for the pastorate. (384)

Laypeople, by and large, agree that the pastor is to have ultimate control of all that transpires in the local church. On reading the remarks of Elaine Costen, a member of the gargantuan First Baptist Church of Hammond, Indiana, one imagines that participants in a door-to-door evangelism program hardly dare decide what shoes to wear without first consulting the pastor:

> Someone chosen by the Pastor should oversee the Ladies' Visitation. Certainly this person will not only be a soul winner, but this leader will also be 100% loyal to the pastor. As the initial plans are laid, every detail should be presented to the Pastor for his approval. Any changes in the future must also be okayed by him. (Hyles 3)

Why do fundamentalists willingly submit themselves to autocratic leadership in their local churches? Quite simply because pastoral authority has been directly linked to the pastor's role as "God's man" conveying the message of God's infallible Word. Richard W. De Haan, of the Radio Bible Class, explains the close connection between the pastor and the biblical text:

> Yes, he is a fallible human being, but God has entrusted His infallible Word to that man. He therefore has a great message to proclaim, and you are under obligation to heed the exhortations and obey the directives which come from the Scriptures through the pastor to you. (*Your Pastor* 18)

Thus pastors are seen not as authorities in their own right, but as conduits of the text. Of course, pastors do not simply recite the scriptures — they interpret and expound them. It is also crucial to recognize that the Bible itself grants authority to extrabiblical agencies: the authority of the text can therefore become at odds with extra-textual authorities mandated, ironically, by the text itself. The authority of pastors and other ecclesiastical figures is supported by Hebrews 13.17; other relevant passages include Paul's pronouncements concerning bishops and deacons in 1 Timothy, chapter 3, and *passim*. We have already seen that fundamentalists effectively equate the Holy Spirit with the text, but to acknowledge the Holy Spirit as teacher and interpreter is to open the door to reader inerrancy with all its consequent threats to institutional and pastoral authority. If one prays for God's help in interpreting the scriptures, one might therefore assume that one's interpretations are correct. Or in the radical words of John:

> But the anointing which ye have received of him abideth in you, and ye need not that any man teach you; but as the same anointing teacheth you of all things, and is truth, and is no lie, and even as it hath taught you, ye shall abide in him. (1 John 2.27)

An essential tension exists between the declaration of John and the statements of the unknown author of Hebrews, Pauline in ideology if not identity. But we are assuming for the present discussion's sake that all scripture is verbally inspired, and it will not do to accept the tension at face value as a difference in emphasis or an outright disagreement between two biblical writers. The fundamentalist Oliver B. Greene offers a clear explanation of how one might negotiate the authority of the individual and that of the institution, while upholding the ultimate authority of the text:

> If the man teaching or preaching is *God's man* he possesses the Holy Spirit; and if *you* are a truly born again child of God *you, too,*

possess the Holy Spirit. Therefore when God's Spirit in the pulpit teaches the pure Gospel, God's Spirit *in your heart* will bear witness that this is true. If there is a question in your mind about the ministry of any man, check his doctrine with the Word of God before you believe him, and let the Word of God be your final authority. (33-34)

Although Greene seems democratic in subordinating pastoral authority to textual authority and granting the individual the right to question the pastor, there are rather dark implications in this model for the ordinary reader. To tell readers to consult the Bible to check a pastor's doctrine is to send them to the text with interpretive model already in hand, one furnished them by fundamentalist authorities. It is a rare person, moreover, who will confidently match his or her Holy Spirit against the Holy Spirit of the pastor. Greene's model works equally well reversed: the pastor can say that his antagonist does not truly possess the Holy Spirit. De Haan acknowledges that some pastors may not be truly called of God (*Your Pastor* 8). But he gives a dire warning to the layperson presumptuous enough to question a pastor's calling: "Tragic can be the result when someone who should know better takes things into his own hands and initiates action against one of God's chosen servants" (22).[9]

It would be misleading to suggest, however, that all fundamentalists are the mental and spiritual slaves of their pastors. Given the high status of the biblical text, it is indeed frequently the case that laypersons will challenge their pastors on doctrinal or quasi–doctrinal points. One of the teens in *God's Choice* disagrees with the church's views on proper church music: "The Bible distinctly says, you know, take trumpets and cymbals and stuff and praise the Lord with that. Over here in Bethany, if you don't have just a piano or organ.... it's wrong, it's a sin, whatever" (Peshkin 241). An outbreak of charismatic behavior in a fundamentalist church can be justified, over the pastor's objections, by citing 1 Corinthians, especially 1 Cor. 14.39 — "Wherefore, brethren, covet to prophesy, and forbid not to speak with tongues." If certain members of the congregation dislike a pastor for whatever reason, they can seize on anything Paul says in 1 Timothy 3 to deem him unfit leadership. Perhaps the pastor's son has been seen drinking a beer; the pastor must be: "One that ruleth well his own house, having his children in subjection with all gravity; (For if a man know not how to rule his own house, how shall he take care of the church of God?)" (1 Tim 3.4,5). Less obviously, how can anyone answer the vague charge that he is not "vigilant" or "sober" enough (1 Tim. 3.2)? Clearly, pastors too can and do suffer at the hands of the text, especially when its readers are given to proof-texting — a habit endemic to fundamentalism, and one which I have just demonstrated in this paragraph. But when a text is inerrant and inspired, in part and whole, proof-texting proves difficult to resist. "In Fundamentalism, a point is commonly established by providing a catena of apposite biblical citations, and heading the list with 'God says so'"(Stevick 50).

These infelicitous combinations of Bible verses notwithstanding, Lowell Streiker argues that the personal knowledge of the Bible enjoyed by most fundamentalists protects them from falling prey to "ultra-fundamentalism," his term for biblicist authoritarian cults (82-83). But as Streiker's observations show, the distinction between fundamentalism and ultrafundamentalism is in degree, not kind:

> The essential teaching of fundamentalism is the claim that the original documents of the Bible were dictated by God to His spokesmen and that everything contained in them is infallible. The innovation added by the ultrafundamentalists is the notion that *their interpretation* of the Bible is equally infallible and, hence, cannot be debated or questioned. The ultrafundamentalist preacher thus becomes as authoritative as God...To question the expositors of the Bible is tantamount to rebellion against God. (98)

Streiker's analysis is excellent; unfortunately, the ultrafundamentalist "innovation" is an inevitability. Interpretation is intrinsic to textual authority. True, most dispensationalists will not automatically consign a non-dispensationalist to hell, but if one insists that the scriptures can be properly understood only through the dispensational scheme, one can logically progress to the claim that such confused readers cannot properly apprehend saving truth. All fundamentalists view the jettison of biblical inerrancy as a threat to Christian faith itself. In *Christianity and Liberalism*, Machen claims that Christian liberalism, which derives from higher criticism of the Bible, is "not Christianity at all" (52).

Thus fundamentalist authorities attempt to keep wayward Bible readers in check. No matter how much one may claim to take the Bible as one's authority, one is judged by one's fidelity to the fundamentalist interpretive model. That allegiance established, it seems that one may apply biblical texts to life circumstances and situations with considerable freedom. And there does exist a certain anxiety among fundamentalists about authoritarian pastors, although expressions of that anxiety do reveal the extent to which authoritarianism is an immanent threat.[10] Paul R. Van Gorder, like De Haan affiliated with Radio Bible Class, chides the pastor who "lords it over" his congregation, and in so doing Van Gorder acknowledges that there are indeed "men who domineer in the church.

They demand from Christ's sheep that which only the Chief Shepherd and Bishop of our souls deserves" (Wiersbe, et al., *Priorities for the Pastor* 27).

Yet Warren Wiersbe's remedy for pastoral highmindedness is nothing short of frightening. In *Priorities for the Pastor*, he enjoins the pastor to humility, admonishing him to remember that it is not he himself, but God, whom he is to represent. Sermons "must not express the opinions of the preacher but the convictions of the Word of God" (8). The pastor must give due attention to personal worship: "As we wait before the Lord in prayer and worship, His Spirit fills us and equips us for ministry" (10). Wiersbe concludes, "Everything we do is but a by-product of our personal fellowship with Him" (15). This exhortation to selflessness, an emptying of self in order to be filled by God's Spirit, can result in an insidious humility, as one believes himself to be, in Fish's words, "just a servant of the text." It is one thing to be autocratic in oneself; it is quite another to be autocratic because one is thus duty-bound as spokesman for the Ultimate Authority. Given a predisposition to authoritarian behavior, it seems a short leap to the personality cults Streiker describes. Indeed, it is far easier to disregard the imponderable claims of a Bhagwan Shree Rajneesh than to resist the exhortations of a Jerry Falwell, who constantly appeals to the authority of a text our culture already reveres, and who, judging by the photo-journalistic record, seems constantly to carry that text on his person — in masterful appropriation of authority by visual identification.

While it is fortunate that many fundamentalist pastors manage to eschew authoritarianism, it is easy to see why they might not. Fundamentalist pastoral theology fosters dictatorial leadership, and its biblical theology furnishes the pastor an inerrant authority with which to identify himself. The evangelical Leslie Tarr, in an attack on "neo-fundamentalism" (by which he means contemporary fundamentalism as opposed to evangelicalism), argues that it bears a "frightening similarity" to cults (46). He demonstrates that scriptural passages such as Heb. 13.17 and 1 Chron. 16.22 — "Touch not mine anointed, and do my prophets no harm" — are used to clinch pastoral authority, and concludes: "Unquestioning loyalty to leadership equated with loyalty to the Lord, yields an authoritarianism that eludes even the modern papacy" (27).

The PBS documentary *Born Again*, an astute and sensitive portrait of an independent fundamentalist church in Massachusetts, reveals the pastor's rule in personal counseling. One parishioner describes how he and his wife rely on the pastor's advice in resolving marital disputes:

> The beautiful thing about having a church where the pastor is a fundamentalist is we can call him up and ask him where in God's Word to find the answer to our dilemma. And we don't call him up

to ask him his opinion — because he's a man the same as I am with as many if not more problems than me. So, you know, what I want to know is where in God's Word I can find the answer. And because he's called of God, he turns around and he can tell me where the passages are in the Bible that pertain to my problem. And let the Holy Spirit answer.

Note the close identification of the pastor and the text, the explicit denial that the pastor's personal opinions are even pertinent. But this pastor does not fare quite so well in mediating the dispute of another couple named Bob and Emma. The couple is estranged; their children are living with Bob, while Emma has moved in with another man. The pastor has been trying for some time to persuade Emma to return to her husband. Finally, he and Bob decide that Emma can no longer see her children until she stops "living in sin." As the pastor puts it to the filmmakers, "I am preaching to Emma through Bob's kids." Despite the anguish this preaching causes Emma, she remains unwilling to reconcile with Bob and eventually seeks a divorce, under which terms she will than have the legal right to see her children.

Having given a brief sense of the issues involved, I want to look closely at two scenes involving the pastor — his final meeting with Emma and his subsequent meeting with Bob — to show how a fundamentalist pastor uses the Bible in personal counseling. The pastor and Emma meet at a restaurant. The meeting begins with prayer, the pastor asking God for insight and wisdom. He tells Emma he is expending so much effort on her situation because "I really believe *God* wants it, *not me.*" He then turns immediately to the Bible, citing 1 Cor. 5.7 to show Emma that her husband is a "new creature" and her boyfriend is not. He tells her, "Get back into a Bible preaching, fundamental church. Please. For your own good. Get back to church and get back into this book. Cause this book [he pats the Bible] is the only thing that's gonna save you." But Emma does not succumb, despite the artful structure of this counseling session, which begins with the invocation of God's guidance for the ensuing discussion and makes use of scripture throughout the conversation.

Cut to the pastor's meeting with Bob. The pastor reports, quite correctly, "It was just like talking to a cement wall." Having previously encouraged Bob in his desire for reconciliation, the pastor now realizes the situation is hopeless. Bob reacts with anger, so the pastor now quotes pertinent Bible verses to him, enjoining him to "rejoice when they persecute you for my name's sake" and asking him, "What does Philippians 4.13 say?" [It says, "I can do all things through Christ which strengtheneth me."] "Don't say you *can't* [accept the situation]," the pastor admonishes. "Say you *won't.*" (In the documentary epilogue, we learn that Bob has left the church, and that Emma has filed for divorce and been granted visiting rights.)

On the one hand, we could condemn the pastor for building up Bob's hopes, harassing Emma, and using the children as pawns for "preaching." We could find his about-face use of the Bible a cynical means of avoiding personal responsibility for his own role as mediator. Or, we could see the situation from the pastor's point of view; he has done exactly what a concerned fundamentalist pastor should do when counseling his flock, and neither he nor God is to blame that Emma has been uncooperative. Because Emma is a free agent, able to obey or disobey God as she pleases, the pastor must now turn his efforts toward helping Bob respond to his dilemma with Christian strength and grace.

Personal counseling, especially family counseling, is a vital part of the ministry of most clergy of whatever denominational persuasion. But what is most striking about fundamentalist counseling is the degree to which it purports to be direct advice from God. If we need to find a villain here, it must be the discourse itself, which does not distinguish between the pastor's *perceived* role in applying pertinent scripture to life situations and his actual role as interpreter and mediator.

I have thus far said little about the Holy Spirit as extra-textual authority, for despite his status as God, he does not fare well when doing battle with pastors and commentators. The Holy Spirit in this scenario effectively equates with the authority of the individual — a person claims to be "led" to interpret the text or to behave in a certain way — how can anyone prove or disprove the claim? Although charismatic and Pentecostal Christians place greater emphasis on the agency of the Holy Spirit — as ever-present spiritual guide and giver of spiritual gifts, notably glossolalia — than do self described fundamentalists, none deny the work of the Holy Spirit, in and through the biblical text.

Within these textual boundaries, fundamentalists are quite comfortable with claiming to receive guidance from the Holy Spirit, guidance gotten by praying for it. What a logician would call plain *argumenta ad ignorantia* are often elevated to vital principles in one's personal life, or to use the fundamentalist jargon, "one's walk with the Lord." As Pat Robertson puts it, "For those who seemingly are not able to discern God's positive direction, I recommend 'negative' guidance. Say, 'Father, I want Your will above all else. Please do not let me miss Your plan and purpose for my life'" (78). Having prayed such a prayer, one can safely assume that God will answer it, and therefore that whatever one does will, barring divine intervention, be God's will by default. But clearly an overemphasis on the subjectivity of divine guidance can lead one astray. Robertson also says, "The best way to know God's will is to be familiar with the Bible. That is because 97 percent of everything you need to know concerning the will of God is in the Bible" (77). The other three percent includes a confirmatory sense of peace and the cooperation of circumstance (78).

"God's will" is, in fundamentalism, utterly specific. Although Emma's case is fairly clear cut — she cannot possibly be "in the will of God" when she is not attending church, evidently not reading the Bible, living with a man not her husband, and an unsaved man at that — other personal decisions having no explicit moral content or whose moral content is prima facie are equally to be prayed about to determine whether one's choice is "God's will." In contrast with the practice of many Christians, the fundamentalist determination of God's will is primarily inductive rather than deductive. In a deductive approach, one might, for example, obey Jesus's general commandment to love one's neighbor as oneself by donating food to a shelter for the homeless or volunteering at a nursing home or helping an elderly neighbor rake her leaves. The idea of asking God whether it is his will that one perform such specific acts would strike many Christians as absurd. Good works are the self-evident practical outworking of Jesus's general commandment. Fundamentalists, however, pray about every specific act they contemplate, seeking the Holy Spirit's guidance in helping them determine God's will. Should I contribute to the United Way? Should I buy this Ford or that Chevrolet? Should I go to the basketball game with John or with Chris? Such worldly questions are not, ironically, considered mundane. The depth of fear attendant to living "outside God's will" is evident in the fundamentalist belief that one could be horribly punished, not in the next life but in this one. One may die an untimely death, one's loved ones may be "taken." In *God's Choice*, a visiting evangelist tells his audience, "I'm afraid to get out of the will of the Lord because I'm afraid he'll put his hand on my two daughters or on my wife. Of course, do things because you love God, but you know God punishes those who get out of his will" (Peshkin 120).[11] Although no one claims that God would so severely punish a girl who is dating the "wrong" boy, there is a strong sense that one never knows where that first date will lead. And God might very well punish the girl who marries outside his will.

As for automobile purchases, we can consider the happy experience of Bob Mumford. Like Robertson, Mumford says three factors must fall into alignment before one can be confident that the Holy Spirit is truly at work:

1. The Word of God (objective standard)
2. The Holy Spirit (subjective witness)
3. Circumstances (divine providence)

[65]

Mumford is careful to recognize the supremacy of scripture: "The written Word of God is the supreme criterion in guidance" (66). To illustrate proper integration of these three criteria, Mumford describes how he was led to buy a new car, having desired one for some time. During his personal devotions, he happened to read Ps. 37.4, which says that if you "delight" in him, God will give you the "desires of thine heart" (1. the Word of God). Upon seeing a particular car, Mumford felt "a quiet sense of peace" (2. subjective witness). Finally, he was able to sell his old car (3. divine providence). He concludes, "I purchased the car and by the time I'd put 50,000 miles on it, it still had cost me only forty dollars in repairs, quite unlike the one I bought outside of God's will, which cost me a fortune in repair bills" (73-74).

Detractors of fundamentalism frequently seize on stories like these, Mumford's being not untypical, as confirmation of the egotism of fundamentalists. God has better things to do than help one buy a car, say critics, and abdication of personal responsibility for one's choices in life, whether mundane or momentous, reflects psychological immaturity. But as pastors — in Wiersbe's model — can credit (or blame) God for what they themselves do, so can laypeople. In her visit to Lynchburg, Frances Fitzgerald was struck by the "moon-child quality" of many Falwell congregants (99):

> If you ask a Thomas Road member "What brought you to Lynchburg?" or "How did you find this house?" the answer will be "God brought me here" or "God found this house for us" — and only after that will come some mention of the family's desire for a warmer climate or of the intervention of a real-estate agent. (96)

Clearly, the ascendancy of the text can be threatened by claims of direct revelation from God. At the same time, I would argue that it is the status of the text itself which helps to generate such phenomena. It goes without saying that the Bible is full of passages exhorting believers to listen to the still small voice of the Spirit. By adding to these scriptural warrants the fundamentalist conception of the inerrant text, one can appreciate how the Bible can function as a holy handbook, a collection of divine sayings which can be applied — sometimes cautiously, sometimes willy-nilly — to practical concerns in the believer's life. Fundamentalist scholars and laypersons alike disport in textual gaps. The great emphasis placed on "what the Bible says" has its analogue in what the Bible does *not* say. Fundamentalists are less inclined to search for, to meditate upon, the spirit of biblical passages, than to examine the letter of the text to determine the minimum required of them and the maximum they can get away with. What is not explicitly forbidden by the Bible is permitted.[12]

I realize I have made a large statement here, one not applicable to the many ethically mature fundamentalists. But I would argue that ethical maturity arises largely in spite of rather than because of the fundamentalist conception of the biblical text. Premillennialism, pressed to its logical conclusion, militates against social action or concern for one's neighbors apart from their "souls." Consider, for example, a reading from the popular daily devotional series *Our Daily Bread*:

> Writing in *Outreach*, a publication of the Oriental Missionary Society, Richard D. Wood raised a thought-provoking question about our motives in supporting missions. He said he has often heard tourists who had just come back from Haiti say, "God broke my heart for missions in Haiti." But he wonders whether these people were moved more by the physical poverty of the Haitians than by their spiritual poverty. Was the lack of physical poverty uppermost in the tourists' minds rather than the Haitians' need for the Bread of Life — the Word of God? Mr. Wood recognizes that God often has to wake us up, and a people's extreme need may be His way. But he wonders if those same visitors to Haiti were to take a stroll through an average middle- or upper-class suburb in America, would they cry, "God broke my heart in the suburbs"? (DeHaan, "Of Jungles")

Nowhere in this short essay does DeHaan express concern for physical and spiritual needs together. The Word of God is not just primary in importance but singular. Physical poverty is merely God's way of "waking us up" to the genuine need of the population.[13] One cannot but respond viscerally to what is, in my opinion, a remarkable callousness here expressed. But if one understands the overriding concern with proper *belief* ("one's eternal welfare depends on what one believes," said Packer, with saying the right words, said Stevick), one can appreciate the way in which the biblical message can be construed as primarily doctrinal rather than moral. Literalism and inerrantism tend to close off rather than creatively expand practical application.

The authority of fundamentalism is indeed constituted in the biblical text, *as that text is interpreted*. Only by concealing their role as interpreters are fundamentalist authorities able to wield their immense power over ordinary believers. Thus one does not question the authority of a DeHaan or a Falwell for to do so is to question God. In Patricia Pingry's short biography of Falwell, Falwell is quoted as saying, "The man who walks with God is indestructible. God's man is indestructible until the day he's finished the work God has called him to do" (37). Falwell's status as God's representative is so solid that his followers ask him to autograph their Bibles

(Pingry 59) — a practice more fitting, perhaps, than it might first appear. Seen in this light, Falwell's conception of church discipline is rather chilling:

> The Thomas Road Baptist Church attempts to get every believer to join the church, hence under the discipline of the Word of God.... The Word of God admonishes those straying to return and repent. Discipline is not found in "consensus" of deacons or of a congregation. This discipline is found in the Word of God and men are judged by it. (Towns and Falwell 49)

John R. Rice also recognizes that church discipline will be ineffective unless the pastor is careful to ground his pronouncements in the Bible. Rice warns pastors against hastily laying down "rigid rules of conduct" for church leaders and teachers: "A pastor needs to have a tender, kindly heart toward people who do not have as much light on these matters as he has, and one needs a proper respect for other people's opinions, even though one does not agree with them" (133-34). Notice the kindly condescension of Rice's tone, continued in his eventual advice on the proper technique for getting one's way with one's congregation. "So, pastor, move with ease and kindliness; prove your points by the Bible; show that you love the people, and take time to sell a matter. Until you can convince the church that you are right and until they willingly, gladly follow you as God's man on a matter, it would not be wise to set up drastic rules" (134).

Depending on the nature of one's own presuppositions about fundamentalist preachers, this passage could easily be taken to confirm their cynicism. Rice's political savvy is stunning, so stunning in fact that one must question whether he himself is truly conscious of what he has wrought. Because Rice is himself a Bible believer, he is heir to a tradition, a participant in a discourse of which he is not the master, of which *no one* is the master. In Foucault's terms, discourse "is not the majestically unfolding manifestation of a thinking, knowing, speaking subject, but, on the contrary, a totality, in which the dispersion of the subject and his discontinuity with himself may be determined" (*Archaeology* 55). That Rice no doubt enjoys the perks of power and experiences personal gratification in his pastoral role is ultimately irrelevant to the matter at hand. Preachers are bound by the rules of fundamentalist discourse, and as subjects, they may occupy different sites and perform different roles according to particular circumstances and events. The limitations on the power of the fundamentalist preacher have been clearly evident throughout the course of the PTL scandal. We have seen the ease with which Jerry Falwell overtook Jim Bakker's ministry, the falling away of financial support for virtually all television ministries, and Falwell's eventual retreat not only from Bakker's PTL ministry but from his own Moral Majority. At every stage, one senses that the farther a fundamentalist preacher strays or is perceived to stray from the Bible, the worse his fortunes among his own followers. A preacher risks losing his power the more he distances himself from the Bible; he enjoys authority only insofar as he represents the Word of God.

In associating his own discourse with the Word of God, the fundamentalist preacher is not only able to get others to take him seriously. He is able to take *himself* seriously. Without the Bible, he is nothing — as Rice himself acknowledges in this reply to a "liberal" critic of his message and methods:

> Non-christians certainly would not be interested in a Christianity which did not have a supernatural Saviour and they would not have much confidence in a preacher who did not have a definite, divinely given message. And in actual practice, as it is very easy to prove, non-Christians are much more likely to be won to Christ by such plain preaching as I do and as the men with whom I associate do, than with the other kind. (173)

What is "plain preaching"? It is preaching that is laced through and through with biblical references. For Rice, the "evangelistic sermon" should follow this formula:

> *The sermon must be definitely scriptural.* Maybe it should be prepared around one verse of Scripture, a text. Sometimes it should be prepared as an expository treatment of a whole passage of several verses. But even if it is a topical sermon, one ought to establish the theme of the sermon directly upon a text or Scripture in the plain meaning of that Scripture, and then one should prove all the subdivisions of the sermon by Scriptures. It should be distinctly a Bible kind of sermon" (385, original emphasis).

Finally, we ask the wrong question when we attempt to discover whether fundamentalism is an authority of the Word or an authority of the preacher. It is both and neither. The biblical text is prescribed by the preacher's interpretations and in turn prescriptive of them. Although preachers are quite forthright in staking their claims to authority, they associate and often equate their authority with that of the Bible. Bible believers are, therefore, hard pressed to challenge the authority of their pastors. Those who do will find their objections deferred again and again to the inerrant Word, the Word in which they themselves believe.

Chapter 7

The Twoedged Sword:
The Doctrine of Hell

*It was Jesus — Jesus whom modern liberals represent as
a mild-mannered exponent of indiscriminate love — it was
Jesus who spoke of the outer darkness and the everlasting
fire.*

J. Gresham Machen[1]

*As the meek and gentle Savior [God] was a thousand
billion times crueler than ever he was in the Old
Testament — oh, incomparably more atrocious than ever
he was when he was at the very worst in those old days!*

Mark Twain[2]

If the power of any discourse derives in some measure from the
quantity and quality of fear it can instill in its subjects, fundamentalism
is supremely powerful in its doctrine of the everlasting, conscious torment
suffered by the unsaved in the literal fires of hell. To comprehend
why fundamentalists hold this doctrine — and how this doctrine holds
them — it is vital to recognize that their doctrine of hell is a direct
consequence of the literalistic interpretation of an inerrant text. Without
that conception of the text, articulation of the doctrine would have little
power; if one is not convinced that the Bible is the inerrant word of God,
and if one does not believe that it "means what it says," one will not
find the classic fire and brimstone sermon a compelling reason to
become — and remain — a fundamentalist.

That such sermons do succeed in persuading converts demonstrates
the extent to which belief in the inerrancy and divinity of the Bible is both
common sense and commonplace, inasmuch as the goal of these
sermons is to convert the unconverted. The converting sinner logically
must recognize the authority of the text before he or she will be moved
by the authority of its expositor. Without such authority, the sermon
becomes little more than a superbly crafted horror story (or horror film,
as we shall see) sufficient to cause nightmares perhaps, but not religious
conversion.

99

If one assumes for the moment that the fundamentalist doctrines and consequent reading of the Bible are correct, one can instantly appreciate the sheer terror evoked by a sermon on hell. Consider these excerpts from a sermon by Curtis Hutson, editor of *Sword of the Lord*:

> There is real fire in Hell. Hell is a literal place — as real as this building.... In Matthew 25:41, Jesus said He would say to some, "...Depart from me, ye cursed, into everlasting fire, prepared for the devil and his angels." ...Why, in your mortal body, you would have a nervous breakdown the first few minutes in Hell. I can't stand the screams in a psychiatric ward. I can't stand the crying and screams at the emergency clinic at the hospital for long without having to leave. In Hell all hope is gone, and those imprisoned there know all hope is gone. Those in Hell know they will never get out, that this is it — ten billion years, ten trillion years, ten billion, trillion years, and they will still be there! (7)

By quoting scripture — and the words of Jesus, at that — Hutson substantiates his own imaginative rendering of hell. Jesus's story of the rich man and Lazarus, in which the rich man cries out to Abraham to send Lazarus to him "that he may dip the tip of his finger in water, and cool my tongue; for I am tormented in this flame" (Luke 16.24), is a popular text. As Robert G. Taylor extrapolates:

> "How awful! How terrible to think of the many in Hell who are screaming for a drop of water to cool their tongues. But, dear lost friend, if you go to Hell, there will be no water. You, too, will scream for a drop to cool your tongue, but you, too, will be denied. (78)

We need not multiply examples endlessly here to ascertain that fundamentalist preachers lack no imagination when construing how everlasting fire will feel, nor is much imagination required given their basic conception of hell. On some occasions, little imagination is required on the part of the audience either, the sermon being supplanted by visual images. In *God's Choice*, a student recounts how she was saved after viewing a film called *Burning Hell*, which, she says, "was trying to make hell as realistic as they can." The realism is, of course, based on literalistic interpretation: "I think, in the Bible it says it's a place where the worm dies not. ...In the movie, it showed the worms were just all over and the people were just all screaming" (Peshkin 208).

As one might expect, children and teenagers are particularly vulnerable to fearsome depictions of hell, whether visual or verbal. I quote excerpts from the late J.C. Ryle's "No More Crying! A Sermon to Children," reprinted in the 26 June 1981 issue of *The Sword of the Lord*:

> In Hell there is no laughter and smiling. There is nothing but "wailing and gnashing of teeth." In Hell there is no happiness. Those who go there cry night and day without stopping. They never go to sleep and wake up happy. They never stop crying in Hell.
>
> I am sorry to tell you, dear children, that there are many people going to Hell. "Broad is the way, that leadeth unto destruction, and many there be which go in thereat." I am afraid that many children are going to Hell. I see many boys and girls who know they are sinners but have never asked Jesus to save them. Where will they go if they die? There is only one other place to which they can go. They must go to Hell. (3)

One might commend Ryle for not being extremely explicit with his tender audience, flames being notably absent from this description, although I do realize that some would say the sermon as it stands equates to mental child abuse. Why would anyone say such a thing to children, or to anyone else for that matter? Are fundamentalists so twisted that they enjoy believing in a literal hell? The majority do not. Ryle himself continues, I think sincerely, by saying, "I cannot bear the thought of boys and girls going to that dreadful place where there is nothing but crying" (3)

That the notion of an eternal, literal hell is a particularly horrifying one hardly bears mention. Why, then, do fundamentalists believe in it? Because the Bible tells them so. There is finally no better illustration of the binding authority of the biblical text than this aspect of fundamentalist belief. It is insufficient to claim that fundamentalists do not care about hell, inasmuch as they themselves will not be going there. Having become convinced themselves of the existence and nature of hell, fundamentalists will quite naturally wish to save others from such a dreadful fate. Despite the remarkably closed worlds in which some fundamentalists live, it is the rare fundamentalist who does not to have at least one "unsaved" relative or friend, whose eternal destiny is therefore of deeply personal concern.

Peshkin's subjects regularly worry about their non-fundamentalist loved ones. A student says he witnesses to his friends, difficult task that it is, "because, you know, I want them to go to heaven and not to hell" (174). A teacher bursts into tears when speaking of her unsaved brother: "I see his children being raised without proper guidance. Some day they'll come to judgment" (118). In the documentary *Born Again*, a young man is unrelenting in witnessing to his alcoholic brother; the brother does eventually walk the aisle. In every case, whether explicit mention is

made of hellfire or not, one senses the almost unimaginable anguish
fundamentalists must feel when contemplating the possible disposition of
those dear to them.[3]

One's "burden for souls," to use the fundamentalist idiom, is not
restricted to one's acquaintances. In many fundamentalist churches there
are designated "soul winning" nights, when church members canvass their
communities seeking to reach the lost through door-to-door visitation.
There are numerous how–to manuals for soul winning on the market, as
well as advice columns in fundamentalist journals. A typical text is the
The Hyles Visitation Manual, by Jack Hyles, pastor of the influential First
Baptist Church of Hammond, Indiana. The manual makes for interesting
reading on various fronts, particularly in its discussion of strategy (it is
advisable to carry a concealable pocket New Testament rather than a large
Bible [176]), its incredible accounts of conversion (conversion seems to occur during the course of only one relatively short visit), and its even more
astonishing statistical claims (the jacket blurb indicates that in 1973 the
church gained 25,044 new members and performed 8,044 baptisms).[4]

Engrossing as these details are, however, my main purpose is to show
how the Bible is used in a fundamentalist's one-on-one encounter with a
potential convert. Like most fundamentalists, Hyles is partial to the book
of Romans, often using a series of salvation verses popularly known as
the "the Roman Road." He recommends that the soul winner ask this crucial
question: "If you died now, do you know that you would go to heaven?"
(194).[5] If the respondent says no, and a large number of Hyles's prospects
do, Hyles says, "If I could take this Bible and explain to you how you could
know beyond any shadow of a doubt.... Would you do what the Bible says?"
(195). At this juncture, the soul winner embarks on the Roman Road,
carefully citing scripture every step of the way:

> Show him that he is a sinner. For this, use Romans 3:10 and 3:23.
> Show him the price on sin. Show him this in Romans 5:12 and 6:23.
> Show him that Jesus paid the price. Use Romans 5:8,
> Show him that Jesus will take us to Heaven if we ask Him in faith.
> Use Romans 10:9-13. (195)

The personal evangelist closely links his or her exhortations with
citations from scripture; in order to avoid conversion, the prospect
therefore must reject not just the message of the evangelist but the
apparent message of God's Word. Whether one believes Hyles's success
stories or not (I do not have independent verification), it seems clear that
those who convert do so because they are persuaded by the Bible. By
selecting which verses will be read, of course, the evangelist performs an

editorial function, naturally avoiding any verses which do not pertain to the purpose, or worse, would seem to contradict fundamentalist soteriology. While we can safely assume that soul-winners are more often than not turned away at the door — the manual, understandably enough, says little of those visits which never develop — it does seem that once a prospect allows the evangelistic message to proceed, conversion frequently occurs.[6] Unlike mainline Protestants or Roman Catholics, fundamentalists offer their prospects immediate and seemingly open access to the Word of God, a technique with telling results. An individual reconverting to fundamentalism describes his first visit to Jerry Falwell's Thomas Road Baptist Church: "When we walked in the front door, that old-time feeling came back. The people were studying from the Bible instead of literature" (Towns and Falwell 19).

But what might be said of the soul winners themselves? To read the *Hyles Visitation Manual* and similar literature is to encounter figures driven to the point of obsession with their task. What compels Hyles "to try to go [soul winning] every Thursday afternoon, every Friday afternoon, and sometimes on Saturday" (171)? That he sets aside specific times for soul winning excursions does not mean that he considers the rest of his time to be time off: he advocates asking everyone one encounters, the neighbor and the meter reader alike, whether they are Christians (172). Yet even an expert like Hyles does not deny the rigors and embarrassments attendant to personal evangelism: "There never is a day when I want to go soul winning.... It never gets easy to ask 'Are you a Christian?'" (170 – 71).

Like new converts, who experience fear for the ultimate destiny of their own souls, mature fundamentalists too are ever cognizant of the horrific fate awaiting unbelievers. Hyles's obsession with soul-winning is an obsession with hell; he is driven by what he reads in his Bible and is thus compelled to attempt to win the soul of everyone he encounters.

Fundamentalists like Hyles are, however, exceptional in their zeal. Thus far too, I have been citing only sources who would not hesitate to call themselves fundamentalists, and about whom few would dispute that identification. Among those who prefer the label *evangelical*, there are significant behavioral and intellectual differences, as well as important similarities.

One does not find in such moderate journals as *Christianity Today* much attention at all devoted to soul winning or the fate of the damned. Among evangelicals, one perceives, once again, that "ethic of civility" (Hunter 152). In this day and age, it is plainly not good form or good taste to tell one's neighbors that they are going to burn in hell if they do not repent. The doctrine of hell is, moreover, plainly repugnant to most moderates. They would not believe it if they did not feel compelled by their Bible belief.

As one of Hunter's subjects, a student at an evangelical college, puts it: "I hope that hell would be like soul sleep — a kind of nothingness — but the Bible doesn't say that" (39). Another says: " The human part of me wants to say that Ghandi would be good enough to get him eternal life, but I think Scripture would indicate that he is not" (38). The only reason these students believe in hell is that they believe the Bible teaches the doctrine.

But where Hunter finds these and similar misgivings about traditional doctrines to be evidence that young people are increasingly uncomfortable with the more rigid and harsh doctrines of their tradition, such misgivings are not by any means the exclusive property of the "coming generation." Such leading lights as Clark Pinnock, who now espouses annihilationism, and Kenneth Kantzer, editor of *Christianity Today*, are clearly disturbed by the fundamentalist conception of hell, yet like their descendants they are bound by the fundamentalism which is a natural consequence of their doctrine of scripture. The subject of hell has been conspicuously absent from the pages of *Christianity Today* in recent years. But this silence was broken in March 1987 with a series of articles on the topic "Universalism: Will Everyone Be Saved?" While discussion centers on the question of whether all humans will be saved — the existence of hell is thus assumed, but potentially rendered pointless by the fact that none will go there — the various contributors implicitly recognize that the nature of hell is inextricably connected with universalist sensibilities. That is, everlasting literal hellfire generates theologizing which attempts to overcome not hell itself, but the fact that anyone will actually experience it.

Because none of these thinkers can find sufficient scriptural warrant for universalism, they instead grapple with the nature of hell.[7] Pinnock, in a bold move, advances the notion that hell is not everlasting — "The 'fire' of God's judgment consumes the lost" — making an essentially political observation: "It is hard enough to defend the Christian message apologetically in relation to the problem of evil and suffering without having to explain this doctrine, too" (40).

Pinnock is subsequently lambasted by David F. Wells, who with considerable justification accuses Pinnock of failing to interpret scripture properly, i.e., fundamentalistically. What of the story of the rich man and Lazarus, Wells asks, where quite clearly the rich man is suffering conscious torment? If the Bible is inerrant — if in other words, Jesus was not misquoted or mistaken on this matter — how can one account for this story? While Wells credits Pinnock's humane sensibilities, he contends that Pinnock's "expressions of moral horror" must eventually be "set on one side so that we can concentrate more clearly on the biblical data" (41). Ultimately, both men bring moral arguments to bear on the question, but where Pinnock finds it inconceivable that God "would install a torture chamber somewhere in the new creation" (40), Wells believes that God's infinite righteousness requires that sin be "infinitely unpardonable" (42).

Some fundamentalists do allow that *fire* may be metaphorical. Pat Robertson, for example, is literalistic enough to note something of a conflict between the biblical descriptions of hell as both "fire" and "outer darkness" (171). Robertson says that the fire may be figural (15), but notes that the damned are conscious in any event (117). But those who allow for figural interpretation usually contend that such a searing metaphor must represent something equally if not even more agonizing than literal fire. The statement of *Christianity Today* contributor Roger Nicole is typical: "The spiritual fire, however, which consumes and sears the soul, is perhaps more terrifying and excruciating than physical burning" (37).

When theologians like Wells and Nicole move beyond reluctant acceptance of this harsh doctrine into attempts to justify its morality — and in Nicole's case, to suggest that the punishment may be even *worse* than literal fire — one does begin to wonder whether there is not some sense in which fundamentalists delight in the doctrine. Joe Edward Barnhart argues that the everlasting conscious torment of non-Christians is a morally reprehensible doctrine, comparing those who defend it to Nazis and Stalinists (175 – 88). "Evangelical theologians who use their talents to rationalize such an unimaginable atrocity are morally comparable to those intellectuals who sank so low in perversity as to write elaborate defenses of the Nazi pogroms" (178). For Barnhart, there can be no justification for this belief; he therefore asserts that believers in hell reflect "the human capacity for rationalizing revenge under the cloak of holy wrath" (180).

On a visceral level, it is difficult to disagree with Barnhart. But it is important to recognize that the fundamentalist doctrine of hell is not, for most fundamentalists, an outlet for their vengeful urges.[8] Wells, I would argue, defends the doctrine because he believes for intellectual reasons that he must. Kenneth Kantzer, who writes a concluding statement to the *Christianity Today* discussion, poignantly reflects the position in which thoughtful believers find themselves. Echoing Hunter's subjects, he says:

> I wish I could say that God is too loving, too kind, and too generous to condemn any soul to eternal punishment. I would like to believe that hell can only be the anteroom to heaven, a temporary and frightful discipline to bring the unregenerate to final moral perfection.

Yet Kantzer is bound to believe otherwise, because he believes in the inerrancy of scripture. He quotes from Matthew 25, where Jesus separates the sheep from the goats, telling the latter, "Depart from me, ye cursed, into everlasting fire." Kantzer quietly comments, in a one-sentence paragraph, "This is our Lord speaking." The word *Gehenna*, Kantzer continues,

> is described as everlasting punishment, everlasting fire, the fire that shall never be quenched, everlasting flames, eternal fire, and so on. That awful word appears 12 times in the New Testament; 11 of those references come from the lips of our Savior.

As we have seen, biblical inerrancy is considered vital to the integrity of Christian faith. One need not agree with this assertion in order to appreciate Kantzer's dilemma. His doctrine of hell follows logically from his doctrine of scripture. To disbelieve in hell, he would have to repudiate his doctrine of scripture — and with it, his Christian faith. Whatever intrinsic value Kantzer's faith holds for him, by rejecting it he would also risk being wrong — and for the individual well-schooled in fundamentalism, the possibility of being wrong carries with it the most unspeakable of consequences.

In the doctrine of literal hellfire, we can see very clearly that the power and authority of fundamentalism are constituted in the ultimate autonomy of its discourse. The doctrine arises from the literal interpretation of an inerrant text. It is expounded by preachers and laypeople alike. Few if any fundamentalists take pleasure in the doctrine. But for its perceived foundation in the Bible, it would not be believed.

Chapter 8

Of the Joints and Marrow: Conclusion

"Truth" is linked in a circular relation with systems of power which produce and sustain it, and to effects of power which it induces and which extends it. A "regime" of truth.

Michel Foucault[1]

For the word of God is quick, and powerful, and sharper than any twoedged sword, piercing even to the dividing asunder of soul and spirit, and of the joints and marrow, and is a discerner of the thoughts and intents of the heart.

Heb. 4.12

The authority of fundamentalism arises from the intricate interplay and complex interrelation of the Bible and those who interpret it. Through its appropriation and management of the Bible, fundamentalism thrives. Its compelling power is a function of its success in portraying itself as the clear and plain exposition of the words of God himself. Its authority grows in the fertile field of common sense. It makes no sense for God's book to have mistakes in it, and the fundamentalist says so. Jesus tells of the rich man who "in hell lift up his eyes" to Abraham, saying "I am tormented in this flame." Who is more credible — the Son of God or the liberal clergyman who denies the existence of a literal hell?

If the doctrines of fundamentalism are harsh, they are nevertheless plain and unambiguous. To the perplexed, fundamentalism offers certainty. To the seeker of knowledge, it offers answers to life's momentous questions. In Francis Schaeffer's words:

With the propositional communication from the personal God before us, not only the things of the cosmos and history match up but everything on the upper and lower storeys matches too; grace and nature; a moral absolute and morals; the universal point of reference and the particulars, and the emotional and aesthetic realities of man as well. (*The God Who Is There* 109)

107

The appeal of Schaeffer's orderly universe is strong. The Bible, he says, offers fulfillment of our deepest yearnings for knowledge of ourselves and our world. Even when we recognize that comprehensive understanding is beyond the ken of any mere mortal, we still fervently wish to believe that somehow, somewhere, in the mind of God, all things are known and all things make sense. This hunger for comprehension need not be perceived as an explicitly religious sensibility. In remarking on "the quite non-religious appetite for belief in a true Book," James Barr has said, "The belief that the Bible has been 'proved true' is not necessarily a particularly religious belief at all: it is widely entertained by people as a form of quite secular credulity.... People like or want to believe that there is somewhere some one book that is absolutely true or correct, and if there is to be such a book, in our society it is likely to be the Bible" (139).

As the tone of Barr's comments suggests, however, our wishing for certainties and true books is believed by some to be unsophisticated, a sign of intellectual weakness and "credulity." It is thus perceived as the province of the naive, the fearful, the untutored. Yet, as Frank Kermode reminds us, none of us, literary critics especially included, have yet lost our very human taste for clarity, order, and unity:

> If there is one belief (however the facts resist it) that unites us all, from the evangelists to those who argue away inconvenient portions of their texts, and those who spin large plots to accommodate the discrepancies and dissonances into some larger scheme, it is this conviction that somehow, in some occult fashion, if we could only detect it, everything will be found to hang together. (*Genesis* 72)[2]

We have already seen that fundamentalists and literary critics share similar techniques and difficulties in interpreting their respective texts. Kermode takes us a step farther, holding up a mirror in which we see reflected our own image and that of some distant cousins we might prefer not to call kin. We have in common the habit of cosmologizing: whether we seek to explain the origins of the universe, or more modestly, the world of a novel, we share what literary critic Edward Said calls "an imaginative and emotional need for unity, a need to apprehend an otherwise dispersed number of circumstances and to put them in some sort of telling order, sequential, moral, or logical" (*Beginnings* 41). The need to interpret arises from our need to make sense of things and it is in that sense a religious impulse.[3] My conclusions about the discourse of fundamentalism are thus made with a profound sense of kinship — with fundamentalist interpreters and ordinary readers alike. All interpreters of texts must struggle with the issue of authority in interpretation; all readers must trust that their leaders and teachers will not abuse that authority.

Situated in the center of the web of fundamentalist discourse is the Bible, its inerrant words the basis both for verifying and justifying commentary external to it. By refusing to allow for the possibility of error in the text and by insisting that the scriptures are to be interpreted literally, according to their "plain sense," fundamentalism attempts to proscribe interpretations threatening to its authority. And this proscription is incumbent on laity and clergy alike. Because the clergy are in positions of power, however, their interpretive authority is correspondingly greater than that of the laity. We have seen that fundamentalist preachers wield their considerable clout by allying themselves with the Bible; their listeners heed both the word and the Word, without being able to tell which is which. To question the pastor or to disagree with him is often equated to disobedience against God.

And the power of the preacher lingers in the text. Once one has been influenced by a particular interpretation of a text, it becomes exceedingly difficult to read the primary text again without reading, at one and the same time, an interpretation once furnished it. One experiences this phenomenon most keenly in fundamentalist discourse, given its equation of the biblical words with the words of God. The sole authority of this primary text, coupled with its inextricable interpretation, results in a profound reverence for the very words of the Bible. These words, in turn, resonate with the voices of those who have spoken them in interpretive contexts. In reading, one hears the voice of the preacher in much the same way as one might see and hear only Laurence Olivier's Hamlet in a re-reading of *Hamlet*. It is well enough to hope that faulty interpretations might be supplanted by more "correct" ones, but it is difficult indeed to still the interpretive voices which give particular inflections to biblical passages.[4]

But if, as I have argued, even the Jerry Falwells and the Pat Robertsons are bound by the impersonal, anonymous, autonomous rules of discourse, we are potentially left in a state of ethical paralysis, clearly aware of the abuses and dangers of fundamentalism yet powerless to criticize the actions of its leaders who are, after all, only obeying the rules of a discourse of which they are not the masters, of which no one is the master. Can we find no one on whom to pin the blame? This question or questions reasonably like it have been raised frequently with reference to Foucault, as even his staunchest admirers recognize that his attitude toward power is, in Edward Said's words, "curiously passive and sterile" (*The World* 221). Does Foucault's theory of discourse prohibit our passing judgment on the actions of individuals? In *Beginnings*, Said applauds Foucault's methodology, saying, "Foucault's archeologies have had the effect of laying bare a logic inherent in knowledge but no longer dependent upon the manipulation of a constantly intervening subject" (314). Yet Said is himself extremely reluctant to let those subjects off the hook of personal responsibility; in *The World, The Text, and the Critic*, he criticizes Foucault for those moments when Foucault's "methodological breakthrough becomes the theoretical trap" (244). Taking Stanley Fish to task on the same point, Said asks, "Is it the inevitable conclusion to the formation of the interpretive community that its constituency, its specialized language, and its concerns tend to get tighter, more airtight, more self-enclosed as its own self-confirming authority acquires more power, the solid status of orthodoxy, and a stable constituency?" ("Opponents, Audiences" 9). Said's own career has been marked by an insistence that authorities must be questioned and oppressive powers challenged, for there is no "spider's web without the spider" (*The World* 221).[5]

Most of us are not content, in short, with mere description. We wish to detect clear causal relationships in order that we might give praise and criticism where each is due. But description can be and must be the first step. By describing the discourse of fundamentalism, one can at the very least expose its interior logic, an exposure vitally necessary to challenging and perhaps defusing its power. Foucault's notorious characterization of power as "intentional and non-subjective," a characterization variously criticized as incoherent and unproductive, is, however, a particularly apt description of the power of Protestant fundamentalism. As Foucault observes, "There is no power that is exercised without a series of aims and objectives. But this does not mean that it results from the choice or decision of an individual subject.... The logic is perfectly clear, the aims decipherable, and yet it is often the case that no one is there to have invented them" (*History* 94 – 95).

Although no one achieves ultimate mastery in and over fundamentalist discourse, all of its participants play — at various times, some more so than others — the dual roles of prince and pawn. To employ our web imagery, we could note that where Jim Bakker was once a rather influential spider, he quite rapidly turned into a large bug snared in the web, his improprieties having clearly transgressed the rules of discourse. Most of us would feel, on the basis of our elusive common sense if not on solid philosophical grounds, that our choices, actions and beliefs are neither completely determined nor completely free. And it is in that space that we might make some final evaluations.

As we have seen, it is difficult and sometimes impossible to distinguish between a text and a particular interpretation of that text. Our critiques of fundamentalism must therefore be tempered with empathy. Those who do not embrace the fundamentalist message have often failed to appreciate the binding power of that message over the hearts and minds of Bible believers. In criticizing the message, one cannot fail to comprehend and respect the situation of the messengers — who, like all interpreters, make their assertions because their text tells them so.

We must recognize that the authority of fundamentalism is compelling. But we can reasonably require of the leaders of fundamentalism a forthright acknowledgement of their role in constituting that authority. Is it possible for a fundamentalist pastor to transcend his discourse enough to recognize that role? The answer must be a qualified yes. For one thing, and this is purely a rhetorical point, fundamentalists themselves routinely expect non-fundamentalists to transcend the boundaries of their various discourses. One is expected to recognize the truth of fundamentalist discourse, and if one does not, one will be punished — if not in this life than certainly, dreadfully, in the next. Second, fundamentalists themselves might recognize that the supposed divinity of their interpretive strategies is not borne out in actual practice: the acrimony with which fundamentalists debate one another not only calls the strategies themselves into question, but the very nature of the strategies exacerbates conflict and fosters arrogance. Parties to conflict believe they have God on their side, and those completely outside the discourse are perceived either as lost souls to be won or enemies to be beaten. Finally, even if the Bible were inerrant, we have seen that inerrancy is ultimately incidental to the way fundamentalist authority is actually constituted. Although it is perceived by fundamentalists themselves to be vital for authority, biblical inerrancy becomes in actual practice a political tool whereby one's questions or objections can be deferred to the text. Not *my* words, we are told, but the inerrant words of God, the literal sense of which one ignores at one's peril. Here, the potential for abuse must be recognized, a potential particularly acute in a discourse which portrays its pronouncements as the word and will of God, denying the interpretive contributions of fallible humans. Protestants and fundamentalists in particular have often accused the Roman Catholic church of authoritarianism, but the Roman church has at the very least been forthright about acknowledging the role of human beings in the constitution of authority — whether in the particular person of the Pope or in the communal authority of ecclesiastical tradition. One stands a far better chance of challenging a revealed authority than a hidden one, and one stands hardly any chance at all when that hidden authority is parading in the guise of holy scripture.

Fundamentalists are by no means alone in their desire for a solid authority on which to base their beliefs and their very lives. But one cannot base that authority on a misplaced faith in an inerrant text free from the taint of human interpretation. Whether fundamentalist or ardent secularist or somewhere in the vast plain in between, all of us do well to interrogate our discourses with rigor and expound our truths with humility.

Afterword

From the earliest conceptual stages of this book, I had determined that television evangelists would not receive extensive coverage. Their public notoriety far exceeding their actual prominence on the fundamentalist landscape, they were erroneously perceived by outsiders as the anointed spokesmen for American fundamentalism, Meanwhile, rank-and-file fundamentalists were where they had always been on Sunday morning — in church listening to their own preachers, not home watching TV. By focusing on comparatively underpublicized figures, I intended to re-adjust our skewed picture of fundamentalism, bringing to light the thought and practice of the many, rather than the spectacular visions of the few.

But the unprecedented and unremitting crises besetting televangelists in recent months do call for a postscript. Virtually every major television evangelist has suffered a serious loss to his credibility. Once the grand old man of televangelism, Oral Roberts is now infamous for his alleged receipt of death threats from God and his later claim to have raised the dead. Jim and Tammy Bakker are, in a word, laughingstocks. Having hurled stones at Bakker, Jimmy Swaggart, it turns out, is not without sin himself. Pat Robertson failed dismally in his presidential bid. And Jerry Falwell, smarting from his involvement in the PTL affair, has retreated to the Lynchburg pulpit where the Religious Right was born, expressing his desire to return to his first calling — preaching and saving souls.

Although the circumstances of these cases have varied widely, there is a common theme to these peculiar stories. Whether consciously or inadvertently, each man had so distanced himself from the sole authority of the Bible that he could no longer lay sufficient claim to pastoral authority. Bakker and Swaggart fell into sexual sins clearly irreconcilable with biblical standards for pastors. Oral Roberts claimed to receive revelations directly from God. Robertson not only ceased appearing on "The 700 Club" but relinquished his ministerial credentials in order to pursue his candidacy for secular office. Long overly involved in worldly matters, Falwell decisively shocked and alienated his fundamentalist core constituency by dabbling in the tangled affairs of charismatics.

If it were true that "great men of God" were the real power on the fundamentalist throne, these evangelists would have been able to weather their personal and corporate crises. It is now more clear than ever that a fundamentalist preacher's authority exists in direct proportion to his ability to identify himself with the Bible. Financial contributions to all television ministries have plummeted. Jim and Tammy Bakker's various attempts to reclaim PTL or start their own ministry anew have been hampered by lack of popular support. Of the lot, Jimmy Swaggart and Jerry Falwell may have the best chance at reversing their fortunes. Unlike Jim Bakker, Swaggart confessed his sin in the time-honored and biblically sanctioned manner, with due sorrow and repentance. His subsequent refusal to accept the discipline mandated by his denomination should not hinder his ability to rebuild his ministry, provided that he is ever careful to claim submission to the higher discipline of God's Word. Falwell, by consciously re-adopting the pose of an ordinary preacher of the Word, appears to have recognized whence his authority truly arises. His current political activities, such as lobbying on behalf of Lt. Col. Oliver North, have been conducted from spiritual headquarters, North giving the 1988 commencement address at Falwell's Liberty University.

While outsiders have viewed the crisis in televangelism with a mixture of condescension and unmitigated glee, fundamentalists have expressed little more than rueful embarrassment. The interpretive community was chagrined and saddened, yet it did not hesitate to relinquish its loyalty toward leaders who had transgressed its rules. The discourse of fundamentalism remains intact, for its authority was never truly threatened. The scandals and setbacks came and went like violent thunderstorms, disturbing the atmosphere but leaving the ground unscathed.

Notes

Chapter 1

1. *Treatise on the Gods,* p. 37.

2. This study does not concern itself with forms of fundamentalism other than Protestant (e.g. Jewish, Catholic, Islamic), although it is certainly possible that it could be relevant to studies of other forms. The reader should understand, however, that when I refer to fundamentalism throughout this work, I mean Protestant fundamentalism specifically.

3. Peshkin spent eighteen months "as a participant in, and observer of" a fundamentalist church and affiliated school in a small Illinois town. The location is not revealed and most of the individuals are identified by pseudonyms.

4. Here and throughout the text, I shall use the masculine singular pronoun when making singular reference to a preacher, pastor or evangelist. With very few exceptions, fundamentalist denominations do not ordain women, and non-sexist pronoun usage would, in this instance, give an inaccurate impression.

5. See Falwell et al., pp. 128–31, for a thorough overview of fundamentalist antagonism toward Graham. While few question Graham's orthodoxy, fundamentalists' main criticism is that Graham errs in not "separating" himself from the ungodly. Ian Paisley, for example, "calls for the complete rejection of Graham and asks Christians to forgive Graham for 'sending converts back to the papal anti-Christ' " (247).

6. These are the usual criteria by which "evangelicals" distinguish themselves from "fundamentalists." Cf. Barnhart's *Southern Baptist Holy War*; fundamentalists are more inclined to believe that only they are true Christians; evangelicals regard fundamentalists as "too exclusivistic," "anti-intellectual," and "unduly preoccupied" with eschatology; fundamentalists are more oriented than their evangelical brethren to the New Testament church model (68).

7. Authorship of any work bearing Jerry Falwell's stamp of approval is problematic, although the problem is immensely revealing of Falwell's perception of his pastoral authority. The title page of *The Fundamentalist Phenomenon* indicates authorship thusly: Jerry Falwell, ed. with Ed Dobson and Ed Hindson. Falwell himself wrote the final chapter. In his foreword, he makes it clear that Dobson and Hindson wrote all the rest, and that they were writing at his request.

When Falwell does not actually *author* works, he very clearly *authorizes* them. Patricia Pingry is the author of the adoring short biography, *Jerry Falwell: Man of Vision*, but Falwell holds the copyright. In *Church Aflame*, co-written by Falwell and Elmer Towns, Towns often serves as a convenient third-person narrator, making remarks which, coming from Falwell himself, would be insufferably immodest. E.g., "To the kids, Rev. Falwell is 'Jerry.' He is close to each one as a buddy, yet they respect him as God's man. The teens flock to their pastor, and many high school boys reflect the feeling of the young preacher boy, Danny Smith. 'The greatest compliment in life is to be called a man of God, the second is to say I am like Pastor Falwell.' Perhaps both compliments are the same" (119).

8. See Charles Farah's useful article, "America's Pentecostals: What They Believe." While some Pentecostals and charismatics strongly emphasize extra-biblical revelation, Farah notes that "when pressed, almost all Protestant charismatics (and certainly all Pentecostals) will insist on the Reformation principle of *sola scriptura*. The formal theology of authority is orthodox, although actual practice sometimes is not" (24). (The distinction between Pentecostal and charismatic, although an important one, is largely irrelevant to my study. Farah provides a useful analysis.)

9. Donald W. Dayton has remarked, "Much intellectual confusion would have been spared if the label 'fundamentalist' had been (properly, I think) maintained" (125). As Dayton notes, the essential theology of fundamentalists and inerrantist evangelicals is the same. Similarly, Hunter regards fundamentalism "as a faction *within* Evangelicalism and not as a movement *distinct from* Evangelicalism" (3–4).

Chapter 2

1. Charles Hodge, "The Inspiration of Holy Scripture," *Biblical Repertory and Princeton Review* 29 (October 1857): 664. Quoted in Marsden, *Fundamentalism*, p. 111.

2. *The Genesis of Secrecy*, p. 144.

3. See, for example, Lonnie Orfitelli, "My Search," *Decision*, Sept. 1986: 4–5. Orfitelli's article is a first-person account of conversion. *Decision* is a monthly magazine published by the Billy Graham Evangelistic Association.

4. I do not, however, provide exhaustive review of these matters. Two valuable book-length studies are James Barr's *Fundamentalism* and Dewey Beegle's *Scripture, Tradition and Infallibility*.

5. Reagan made this statement on 4 February 1985. The *Washington Post* subsequently reported on 22 February that the president defended his use of scripture by observing that the Bible "contains an answer to just about everything and every problem that confronts us" and further said he had checked his usage of Luke 14.31 with "a few theologians" and "they seemed to think it was perfectly fitting, yes. It was a caution to those people in our country who would, if given the opportunity, unilaterally disarm us" ("Reagan Defends Use of Scripture").

Chapter 3

1. *Alleged Errors and Discrepancies*, p. 17.

2. Trinity Baptist College (Jacksonville, Florida), advertisement, *Sword of the Lord* 5 June 1981: 7.

3. For further reading on the Princeton theologians and their place in American church history, see Sandeen pp. 114–131, and Marsden pp. 109–118 and *passim*. For Sandeen, dispensationalism and the Princeton theology are the parents of modern fundamentalism. Marsden argues that the Princeton theology flourished due to the influence of Scottish Common Sense Realism and Baconian notions of science. Marsden's essay, "Everyone One's Own Interpreter?", is a good short overview of his thesis (Hatch and Noll pp. 79–100). Barr's critique of the Princeton theology (261–70) highlights the essential problems inherent in the inerrancy doctrine; Beegle mentions Princeton figures here and there in passing, but there is no centralized critique. Whether credited or not, Packer's defense of inerrancy has been highly influential in succeeding modern works. Lindsell is editor emeritus of *Christianity Today*. I cite Lindsell frequently for two other reasons as well. As he himself says, the *Battle for the Bible* is written for the laity (13); a crucial part of this study is investigating how fundamentalist doctrine is formulated for and understood by the rank and file. Finally, I admire his consistency. Although Lindsell is sometimes criticized by those who fancy themselves more scholarly than he (Archer, for example, finds Lindsell's postulation of six Petrine denials an "unsatisfactory" resolution of a Synoptic discrepancy [65]), it is precisely Lindsell's often untraditional solutions to textual problems which show a truly inerrantist —and literalist — mind at work.

4. E.g., the editors of the *New Scofield Reference Bible* state in their introduction: "This is an appropriate place to assure the reader that, in common with Dr. Scofield and his associates in the original work, every member of the committee of revision believes in and teaches the plenary inspiration and inerrancy of the Scriptures; the triune Godhead composed of the Father, the Son, and the Holy Spirit; the virgin birth and Deity of Christ", etc. (v). See also the 1878 Niagara Creed (Sandeen 273); *God's Choice* — for the American Association of Christian Schools Statement of Faith (303) and the Employee Contractual Agreement (307); in short, the creeds of fundamentalist churches, colleges, and para-church organizations everywhere. I would state unequivocally that any creed which mentions the Bible before it mentions God is by definition fundamentalist.

5. According to 1 Sam. 21.1, the high priest was Ahimelech; according to Jesus, as recorded in Mark 2.26, it was Abiathar. Fundamentalists find this discrepancy especially troublesome in that it involves not only textual inerrancy, but the possibility of error on the part of Jesus.

6. The dictation issue is largely irrelevant to this study, inasmuch as it is a theological one having to do with the methodology of inspiration. I want to note, however, that to read widely in twentieth-century fundamentalist literature is to encounter violent protests, tantamount to rants, against equating verbal inspiration

and dictation. Given the fundamentalist emphasis on God's authorship of the biblical text, I am at a loss to explain either the recurrence or the rigor of this protest, nor have I encountered any such explanations in my research. Hans Frei, however, discusses the issue in *The Eclipse of Biblical Narrative*, and argues that resistance to dictation derives, in effect, from deist infection. Such intellectual virtues as "rationality" and "historicity" came to color the thinking of conservative biblical scholars, and dictation came to be seen as undesirably mysterious and enthusiastic (88–92). Given the marked rationalism and empiricism of contemporary fundamentalists, this seems a plausible explanation. But there is no evidence in the primary material that fundamentalists are aware of why exactly they are against dictation, nor am I aware that they were influenced by the eighteenth- and nineteenth- century European controversies of which Frei writes.

7. See Barr 72–85 for his criticism of regarding Jesus as an expositor of biblical inerrancy.

8. Packer is not a dispensationalist, but compare the dispensationalist privileging of the New Testament epistles over the gospels, pages 51 – 52 below.

Chapter 4

1. *Validity in Interpretation*, p. 230.

2. *The Genesis of Secrecy*, p. 10.

3. For thorough historical studies of Darby-Scofield dispensationalism see Timothy Weber's *Living in the Shadow of the Second Coming*, and Ernest Sandeen's *The Roots of Fundamentalism*. George Marsden also discusses dispensationalism in *Fundamentalism and American Culture* 51–71, and *passim*. Barr's perceptive critique of dispensationalism can be found in *Fundamentalism* 190–207. For short overviews of dispensationalism, see also: Gritsch 15–21; Streiker 97–112; and Falwell, ed. 71–75. See Sandeen 222–24 for his account of the *Scofield Reference Bible*, "perhaps the most influential single publication in millenarian and Fundamentalist historiography" (222). See Barr 191–95 regarding Scofield's Bible, the "influence" of which has been "historically enormous" (191). Of potential interest to literary critics is Kenneth Burke's occasional use of the Scofield commentary in *The Rhetoric of Religion* (see pages 177, 216, 224 and 236). While Burke finds some interpretations convincing and others not, he seems unaware of Scofield's dispensationalist theology.

4. These issues are treated throughout *Fundamentalism*, but see especially pages 40–89 for Barr's distinction between literalism and inerrancy. Too, the co-authors of *The Fundamentalist Phenomenon* (ed. Jerry Falwell), Ed Dobson and Ed Hindson, correctly note that Barr's *Fundamentalism* is restricted "almost totally" to British evangelicalism "which American Fundamentalists do not accept as real Fundamentalism." But, in the end, there is little significant theological difference "since their theology reduces down to biblical inerrancy in any case" (224).

5. For furthur discussion of the rationalist and empiricist impulses in contemporary fundamentalism see Barr, especially pages 235–59 where Barr analyzes the fundamentalist's consequent bias against miracles.

6. See "Normal Circumstances and Other Special Cases," *Is There a Text in This Class?* 268–92.

7. Moreover, certain fundamentalists express strong reservations about allegorizing. See, for example, Packer 102–06, and Walter C. Kaiser, Jr., "Legitimate Hermeneutics," Like Handelman, Kaiser opposes allegorization on grounds that it is not scriptural but Platonic.

8. Although Barr personally believes that "the concept of heresy has ceased to be functionally useful" (197), he says, "If dispensationalism is not heresy, then nothing is heresy" (196). He elaborates, "Christ appears no longer in the role of a saviour calling all men to him but rather as a kind of automaton or switch, whose actions introduce each new stage of the apocalyptic sequence" (205).

9. The dispensationalist eschatological scheme is complex and a more extensive discussion of it is beyond the scope of this work. Its complexity is equalled only by its fascination, and I would recommend study of premillennialism to any student of human behavior or "mythopoeic fantasies." Either the original *Scofield Reference Bible* or the *New Scofield* is a valuable primary source; see also Scofield's *What Do the Prophets Say?* and *Rightly Dividing the Word of Truth.* The best secondary source is Weber's *Living in the Shadow of the Second Coming* —an excellent account not only of premillennialist history but of the effects of such belief on one's behavior. Sandeen's *The Roots of Fundamentalism*, to which Weber is indebted, is the ground-breaking work on this topic, inasmuch as it not only illuminated but adequately defined premillennialism; while the entire work is relevant *passim*, see especially pp. 59–80 for an account of Darby's theology. Marsden criticizes Sandeen for overemphasizing the influence of premillennialism and dispensationalism in the shaping of fundamentalism thought (200–01); however, he does not deny its influence, giving a helpful discussion of dispensationalist eschatology in *Fundamentalism and American Culture*, pp. 48–71.

10. There are two other theological positions having to do with the actual occurence of the millennium and its timing. *Amillennialists* do not believe in the literality of this period at all. *Postmillennialists* believe that the Second Coming of Christ will occur after the millenium; that is, mankind will, with the help of God, progress toward this period of material and spiritual bliss without direct supernatural intervention. Their view of human history, is, therefore, optimistic. *Millenarian*, a term used by some scholars, I take to be synonymous with *premillennial*, although it is sometimes used as a term for millennialist visions in general. Although definitions of these terms can be deduced from many sources, see Weber 9–11 for a good synopsis. See also Weber 274 and 277 for lists of "predominantly premillennialist denominations" and dispensationalist theological seminaries, respectively.

11. Coming from a nascent presidential candidate, this is a startling statement. It is found in Robertson's book, *Answers to 200 of Life's Most Probing Questions,*

published in 1984. Robertson further remarks that "all we can do is be strong enough to restrain the evil that is among us. To do anything other than that is utopian and based upon wishful thinking rather than reality" (9). Also of interest are Robertson's views on demons; e.g., "Undoubtedly Adolf Hitler and Karl Marx were both demonized" (82). The nation's mayors may be particularly interested in this assertion: "It is possible that there is a demon prince in charge of New York, Detroit, St. Louis, or any other city. You find particular sins are endemic in certain cities. One city might have rampant homosexuality, while another might be troubled by excessive lust" (82).

12. See Weber 211–22 for a helpful discussion of Lindsey.

13. Marsden offers some interesting clues, if one can extrapolate from his study of late nineteenth– and early twentieth– century evangelicalism. Marsden has consistently emphasized the *pietist* parentage of evangelicalism. "Although the new dispensational premillennialism was the chief *distinguishing* trait of one side of the movement, it was not even for them the overwhelming controlling interest. Evangelism came first. This evangelistic commitment was shaped by an older set of ideals and assumptions which characterized the pietistic American evangelical revivalism in the era around the Civil War. This older tradition was in many respects culturally optimistic and reformist" (128). Marsden has also observed that premillennialists were themselves quite comfortable with the secular values of the middle class: "Despite the hopeless corruption of the world, there was no demand to abandon most of the standards of the respectable American middle-class way of life. It was to these standards, in fact, that people were to be converted" (38). Perhaps now that middle-class values are no longer entirely "respectable" (viz. the legalization of abortion, tolerance for homosexuality, etc.) modern premillennialists find themselves unable to practice the accommodation of their forebearers.

14. One might also actively assist the fulfillment of premillennialist prophecy. See Weber 179 for an amusing but rather disturbing account of a meeting between Mussolini and two premillennialist interviewers. Mussolini, the story goes, was most intrigued when he learned that the Bible "prophesied" the revival of the Roman Empire. See also Barnhart 171–72 and Robert I. Friedman's article "Terror on Sacred Ground" (*Mother Jones* Aug./Sept. 1987: 36–44) regarding premillennialist efforts to rebuild the temple on Temple Mount in Jerusalem.

Chapter 5

1. "Interpreting the *Variorum*," *Is There a Text in This Class?* p. 173.

2. In this same passage, Fish draws an explicit parallel between literary and religious interpretive practices, noting that Augustine's "rule of faith" is a "rule of interpretation" (170).

3. Beegle (148–49) makes a similar point, noting that scholarly discoveries and insights have caused frequent redefinitions of *inerrancy* over time.

4. Although John R. Rice has much praise for the *Scofield Reference Bible*, he feels free to take issue with it on some points. This is one of them: the gap theory is a "defensive theory" and an "unnecessary concession to scientific thoughts" (461).

5. Multiplying events to achieve harmonization of the scriptures is not a fundamentalist invention. See, for example, Frei's brief discussion of Pietist harmonizations (159–60), and Barr 55–59 for what Barr calls this "most thoroughly laughable of all devices of interpretation" (57). In noting that harmonization is, of course, a function of literalistic interpretation, Barr demonstrates that literalism will be dropped in favor of textual inerrancy at exactly the point when the postulation of certain multiple events becomes too ludicrous even for fundamentalists.

6. See also Barnhart 46–52 for an account of the mental gymnastics Southern Baptists perform with regard to Hebrews 6.4–6, a passage which appears to contradict the Baptist doctrine of "eternal security" or "once-saved-always-saved" (a doctrine derivative of the Calvinist doctrine of the perseverance of the saints).

7. See also Mark Twain's "Letters from the Earth" for a thoroughgoing attack on Christianity, an attack grounded on literalistic Bible reading. Note particularly his account of the Flood which begins humorously ("Another day was lost in getting the flies aboard, there being sixty-eight billions of them.") and rapidly turns to terror ("the multitude of weeping fathers and mothers and frightened little children who were clinging to the wave-washed rocks in the pouring rain....") (29); and his lampooning of belief that God, in the person of Christ, was "sweet, and gentle, merciful, forgiving.... Whereas it was as Jesus Christ that he devised hell and proclaimed it!" (46).

8. Cf. Gerald Graff, "The Pseudo-Politics of Interpretation." Graff argues that literary theories are, in themselves, politically neutral. Specifically regarding Hirsch, "To call Hirsch's theory authoritarian is to assume that such a theory lends itself to one and only one kind of political use and that that use can be determined a priori" (603).

9. See also Pinnock's article " '...This Treasure In Earthen Vessels': The Inspiration and Interpretation of the Bible." "I have always felt that, while inerrancy is not a necessary term, when applied to the whole Bible it does express a firm confidence in the truthfulness of Scripture. The difficulty with it comes when we read into the term suppositions that go contrary to the observed character of the text" (18). These suppositions include "modern standards of, say, historical or scientific writing" (18).

10. There is some lack of clarity and consensus on the relative meanings of these terms. Barnhart's definition is useful: "Inerrancy asserts that the Bible in its original documents is totally without error. Infallibility stresses that the Bible is unfailing in accomplishing the purpose that God intended" (38). But cf. Lindsell: "There are some who try to distinguish between these words as though there is a difference. I do not know of any standard dictionary that does not use these two words interchangeably" (27). Generally speaking, evangelicals who wish to uphold

the ultimate authority of scirpture but, like Pinnock, choke at the logical and phenomenological implications of *inerrancy* will refer to the Bible's *infallibility*. See, e.g., Gabriel Fackre, "The Use of Scripture in My Work in Systematics," Johnston 200–26.

11. Two evangelicals expressing similar views are Roger Lundin ("Our Hermeneutical Inheritance") and Donald G. Bloesch ("A Christological Hermeneutics"). Lundin, an English professor, urges evangelicals to give due recognition to tradition, although he terms Fish's interpretive communities "seductive but lonely worlds" (28). Despite his thoughtful and useful approach, Lundin finally makes what is to my mind a problematic distinction typical of evangelicalism and fundamentalism: "we must ask how to determine whether that which molds the life of a given Christian community is actually the Bible or simply a particular interpretation of the Bible" (81). Bloesch rather nicely fuses authorial intention and the role of the interpretive community — notions which are presently at political if not logical odds — by observing that the scriptures were written in a "community of faith." Only if "we share this faith" of the human authors can we properly understand the scriptures (101).

12. This aspect of Hirsch's theory becomes very interesting when applied to biblical exegesis, fundamentalist or otherwise. Is the authorial consciousness that of God or the human writer or both? For the inerrantist Walter C. Kaiser, Jr., it is the human writer: "To interpret we must in every case reproduce the sense the Scriptural writer intended for his own words" (118). Kaiser then cites Hirsch on meaning and significance. Likewise, Carl F. H. Henry, specifically citing Hirsch: "We must insist that ideally the interpreter shares the objective meaning of the inspired biblical writers" (4.315). Although I am not aware of any fundamentalist sources citing Hirsch to advocate sharing *God's* objective meaning, such arguments may well have been made, and in any event, it seems a logical inference. And consider the remarks of Hirsch himself: "The 'senus plenior,' a conception in scriptural interpretation under which the text's meaning goes beyond anything the human author could have consciously intended, is, of course, a totally unnecessary entity. The human author's willed meaning can always go beyond what he consciously intended so long as it remains within his willed type, and if the meaning is conceived of as going beyond even that, then we must have recourse to a divine Author speaking through the human one. In that case it is His willed type we are trying to interpret, and the human author is irrelevant" (*Validity* 126).

13. Fish's remarks are made with reference to a Shakespeare scholar who says of the sonnets, " 'I mean to describe them, not to explain them.' " This critic's " 'back-to-the text' " stance (Fish's quotation marks) is a typical move "performed when the critical history of a work is deplored as so much dross, as an obscuring encrustation" and it "trades on the assumption, still basic to the profession's sense of its activities, that the function of literary criticism is to let the text speak for itself. It is thus a move drenched in humility" etc. (353).

14. It is useful to compare Henry's reading of Barr with what Barr actually says. E.g., "Indeed, from the errancy of the Bible Barr moves on to the declara-

tion that God's nature is imperfect, that God is vacillating and changing, and that we must repudiate the view that he operates 'out of a static perfection' " (Henry 4.51). Barr: "In the Bible God is presented above all as active and personal: he can change his mind, he can regret what he has done, he can be argued out of positions he has already taken up, he operates in a narrative sequence and not out of a static perfection. The picture of God which presents perfection as the essence of the doctrine of God is clearly of Greek origin and is well represented in the Platonic and Aristotelian traditions" (277). Clearly, Barr and Henry have serious philosophical and theological differences over the nature of God, but just as clearly, Barr's God is not the wimp of Henry's polemical caricature.

15. For this reason, Peshkin had great difficulty locating a school willing to allow itself to be studied by an outsider (11–18). First Corinthians 2.14 was lobbed at him more than once; e.g., one pastor who refused him access "admonished me with 1 Corinthians 2:14, saying that because I do not have spiritual discernment, I will not understand his Christian school" (18).

Chapter 6

1. Packer, *"Fundamentalism" and the Word of God*, p.73.

2. From his sermon "The Day of Great Men Has Not Passed." Quoted in Fitzgerald, p. 96.

3. Weber's "The Two-Edged Sword: The Fundamentalist Use of the Bible" (Hatch and Noll 101–120) gives an excellent short overview of inerrancy and dispensationalism, especially as these hermeneutical principles are supplemented by institutional authority.

4. See Harry S. Stout's "Word and Order in Colonial New England" (Hatch and Noll 19–38) for an illuminating historical parallel — that of the commentary-laden Geneva Bible. The conflict between the Massachusetts Bay authorities and Anne Hutchinson is in part traceable to their use of different Bibles; Hutchinson uses the Geneva, and the authorities the KJV. Stout argues that the individualistic and pietistic tenor of the Geneva commentary was ill-suited to statecraft, hence the ascendancy of the King James in Puritan New England. And Stout's remarks on the anxiety of the early Protestant Reformers are equally relevant to fundamentalism today: "Protestant churchmen believed they were already taking risks simply in making Bibles available to the masses and encouraging their active use.... To provide this Word raw, with no interpretive guidance, would be socially and spiritually reprehensible. It would encourage readers to think they were also their own interpreters of Scripture.... While the people could and must read their Bibles, they could not interpret them independent of ministerial guidance" (22).

5. Despite its date (1964), Stevick's work offers a wealth of currently applicable information about fundamentalist practice, e.g., church polity, mores, the structure of worship services. Although it is unfortunate that no comparable contemporary study exists, the continuing validity of Stevick's study is valuable

in itself and also demonstrates the remarkable stasis of fundamentalism. Peshkin's *God's Choice* and the PBS documentary *Born Again* are not comparable works, for reasons of focus and form respectively, but they do serve to validate the continuing currency of Stevick.

6. Barnhart's source is Odle's "The Bible and Baptist Literature" in William A. Powell, *The SBC Issue and Question* (Buchanan, GA: Baptist Missionary Services, 1977), 164. Barnhart views Odle's statement here as "a show of elitism" (34).

7. For further primary reading on the "chain of command," see, for example: Christensen, Larry. *The Christian Family*. Minneapolis: Bethany Fellowship, 1970. See also Fitzgerard 74 and Fackre 75 for brief but informative discussions.

8. These statements are made within the context of a discussion on the hiring and firing of church staff members, but they reflect general practice in all spiritual and administrative matters.

9. I am unable to elaborate on what tragic consequences De Haan has in mind, nor can I cite from written primary sources any explicit references to divinely prescribed mishaps or outright death visited upon those who take action against their pastors. I have, however, heard certain fundamentalist pastors state in sermons or conversation that evils befalling recalcitrant parishioners were divine judgments. And see page 93 below regarding death and other disasters as divine judgments on those "outside the will of God."

10. Two evangelical sources concerned with authoritarianism are: Mark A. Noll, "Evangelicals and the Study of the Bible"; and David F. Wells, "The Nature and Function of Theology" (Johnston 175–99).

11. See also Peshkin, pp. 173, 195, 211, and 231–32 for examples of fearing God's punishment of self or explaining the misfortunes of others as divine chastisements.

12. I am convinced of the validity of this point, and regret that I am unable to prove it — reasoning of this sort on moral questions does not tend to appear in print. Sexual ethics is a good example. The Bible forbids fornication and adultery, both defined literally (as we must) as sexual intercourse outside the bonds of marriage. Since the Bible says nothing of other heterosexual practices, I have heard unmarried fundamentalists contend that they are free to engage in such "everything but" practices as oral sex and mutual masturbation. Although *The Coming Generation* does not provide conclusive evidence of this sensibility, I would note Hunter's findings on this subject. Ninety-seven percent of students surveyed believe "extramarital sexual intercourse" is "morally wrong all the time." Eighty-nine percent say the same for "premarital sexual intercourse." However, the percentages fall to 45% for "heavy petting" and 23% for "casual petting." Hunter comments, "The biblical injunctions against fornication and adultery are particularly clear, and thus, rationalizing any deviation from these norms would be especially difficult" (59–60).

Although Stevick does remark briefly on the legalistic ethics of fundamentalism — things are either black or white (58–59) — he does not show how the grey is rendered either black or white according to the individual's desires. Fundamentalist pastors and teachers tend to get mightily annoyed with such devious hermeneutical craftsmanship, but given how they teach people to read the Bible, they cannot be surprised by the logic of this approach. Harold Lindsell, in *The World, the Flesh, and the Devil*, offers fairly traditional fundamentalist ethical advice, the first piece being, of course, to see whether the Bible has anything explicit to say about a practice. About practices on which the Bible is silent, he says one should be guided by such criteria as whether Jesus would do it, or whether it might harm one's Christian testimony (160–64). But objectivity is lost, and an authoritative figure can only *contend* that Jesus would not drink beer or attend heavy metal concerts. Fundamentalist children and teenagers, well-schooled in the textually-based "objectivity" of their religion, can become quite adept at disobeying human authorities by appealing to the ultimate authority of the Bible.

One would think that *God's Choice* would offer ample evidence of this dynamic, if indeed it exists. There are a few hints — on pages 197, 225, and 226, students observe that the Bible does not forbid, respectively, "touching a guy accidentally or hitting him," interracial marriage, or dancing. Although I consider *God's Choice* an excellent and accurate study of a fundamentalist institution, I also must wonder to what extent Peshkin's subjects were "witnessing" to him in their interviews and responses to questionnaires. As he notes, he is himself Jewish and his subjects know him to be not only a non-fundamentalist but a non-Christian. Peshkin alludes to his subjects' persistent attempts to evangelize him, but he does not speculate on the extent to which his data may reflect this same concern for his soul; on the contrary, he says, "I am most persuaded of the authenticity of student responses....They knew that we were not Christians, that we were trustworthy, and that they did not have to put on the spiritual dog for us" (174). It seems entirely conceivable, however, that subjects might not be totally candid when such candor would be perceived as detrimental to the strength of their witness to an unbeliever.

13. Stevick finds the same reasoning in his research: "I have known some cases in which contributions to charitable efforts of a nonreligious sort were conscientiously withheld on the ground that the only proper business for a Christian is 'saving souls' " (205).

Chapter 7

1. *Christianity and Liberalism*, p.84.

2. "Letters from the Earth," p.46.

3. This anguish must be particularly acute for converts with "unsaved" loved ones who are already dead. Their conversion will necessarily involve accepting the fact that their loved ones are beyond hope, suffering even now the excruciating pangs of hell. Consider this case, described with a remarkable lack of sympathy

by Mrs. Beverly Hyles, wife of the Rev. Jack Hyles. Mrs. Hyles and her partner in soul winning have engaged a stranger in conversation: "She quickly told us about her husband's very recent death. Of course, we recognized this as an excellent opportunity to witness to her. I asked my trainee, Barbara Taylor, to show her how she could know that if she died, she would go to Heaven. When Barbara had finished, the lady seemed hesitant to receive Christ until we reminded her that if her husband could come back at that moment, he would urge her to be saved. She quickly asked Jesus into her heart and was sweetly saved" (Hyles 95–96).

4. *The Fundamentalist Phenonemon* (Falwell, ed.) reports that attendance at Hyles's church averages 15,000 (141).

5. Sudden-death stories are a staple of evangelistic sermons. This brief narrative, from Hugh F. Pyle's sermon, "One More Night with the Frogs," is typical: "In a Tennessee city a lady heard me preach. She had told the pastor and others that she ought to come forward in the revival. She had never made a public profession of faith. She sat in the service. She heard the Gospel. She raised her hand for prayer. But she did not come forward.

"The next day at noon the pastor was called from the dinner table, an emergency. That woman had been rushed to the hospital late that morning and had died just before noon! Tomorrow may never come!" (15).

6. But cf. Peshkin for a less glowing report of soul winning: "Teachers have come to expect unanswered knocks and partially opened doors, as well as invitations to enter. 'Catholics are the toughest; they don't even want to talk to you when you say you're Baptist' " (68).

7. The Reformed theologian Neal Punt comes the closest, espousing "biblical universalism," which in a nutshell asserts that "those who will be lost are those and only those who, in addition to their sin in Adam, finally persist in refusing to have God in their knowledge" (43). Punt's book-length exposition of his position is *Unconditional Good News* (Grand Rapids: Eerdmans, 1980).

8. AIDS, however, may be a different story. Virtually all fundamentalists believe homosexual practice is a gross sin, and some have explicitly or implicitly stated that AIDS is God's judgment on homosexuals. Before the AIDS crisis, Jerry Falwell wrote in a fundraising letter dated 13 August 1981, "With God as my witness, I pledge that I will continue to expose the sin of homosexuality to the people of this nation. I believe that the massive homosexual revolution is always a symptom of a nation coming under the judgment of God" (quoted in Young 307). Now that the AIDS crisis is upon us, Falwell has new ammunition. The cover of the May 1987 *Liberty Report* (formerly the *Moral Majority Report*) reads:

AIDS?

And in the same way also the men abandoned the natural function of the woman and burned in their desire towards one another, men with men committing indecent acts and receiving in their own persons the due penalty of their error.

Romans 1:27 New American Standard

The evangelist David Wilkerson, writing in the October 1987 issue of Jimmy Swaggart's magazine *The Evangelist*, is unequivocal in stating that AIDS is a divine plague: "It is Deuteronomy 28 being fulfilled to the letter" (14). Although most moderates believe homosexual behavior is sinful, they are, however, reluctant to view AIDS as divine judgment; *Christianity Today* has consistently shown little enthusiasm for this view. See, e.g., Ben Patterson's editorial, "The Judgment Mentality" (20 March 1987: 16–17) and Philip Yancey's gentle and thoughtful essay, "We Have No Right to Scorn" (15 January 1988: 72).

Chapter 8

1. "Truth & Power," p. 74.

2. By *evangelists* Kermode means the writers of the gospel texts.

3. This state of affairs has not gone unnoticed by literary critics, but where Hirsch happily compares his belief in determinate meaning to theism, Jonathan Culler is alarmed by the "complicity" of comparative literature with religion ("Comparative Literature and the Pieties" *Profession* 86: 30–32) and Edward Said asserts that the profession's reverence for its canonical texts cloaks "a guild solidarity that dangerously resembles a religious consciousness" ("Opponents, Audiences" 17).

4. Giving practical help to unhappy fundamentalists and guilt-ridden ex-fundamentalists by showing that the fundamentalist interpretation of the Bible is faulty is, however, the laudable purpose of James Barr's *Escaping from Fundamentalism* (London: SCM, 1984), a work he calls a "pastoral" sequel to *Fundamentalism*.

5. Said's work in general and his two essays "Criticism Between Culture and System" (*World* 178–225) and "Traveling Theory" (*World* 226-47) in particular, have been helpful in my own grapplings with Foucault on this point.

Works Cited

Archer, Gleason L. "Alleged Errors and Discrepancies in the Original Manuscripts of the Bible." Geisler 57–82.

Bahnsen, Greg L. "The Inerrancy of the Autographs." Geisler 151–93.

Barnhart, Joe Edward. *The Southern Baptist Holy War.* Austin: Texas Monthly P, 1986.

Barr, James. *Fundamentalism.* Philadelphia: Westminister, 1977.

Bates, Leon I. *Projection for Survival.* 3rd Ed. Sherman, Texas: Bible Believers' Evangelistic Association, 1980. First published 1977. This edition is the 4th printing, and the 3rd "revised and updated" version.

Beegle, Dewey M. *Scripture, Tradition, and Infallibility.* Grand Rapids: Eerdmans, 1973.

Bloesch, Donald G. "A Christological Hermeneutic: Crisis and Conflict in Hermeneutics." Johnston 78–102.

Born Again. Dir. and Prod. James Ault and Michael Camerini. PBS Special. WNED, Buffalo. 22 Sept. 1987.

Burke, Kenneth. *The Rhetoric of Religion: Studies in Logology.* 1961. Berkeley: U of California P, 1970.

Ciardi, John, trans. *The Inferno.* By Dante Alighieri. New York: Mentor-New American, 1954.

Cole, Stewart G. *The History of Fundamentalism.* 1931. Hamden, CT: Archon Books, 1963.

Dayton, Donald W. "The Use of Scripture in the Wesleyan Tradition." Johnston 121–36.

DeHaan, Richard W. *The Charismatic Controversy.* Grand Rapids: Radio Bible Class, 1978.

———"Of Jungle and Suburbs." *Our Daily Bread.* November-December 1986: devotional reading for 25 November (N. pag.). (Grand Rapids: Radio Bible Class.)

———*Your Pastor and You.* Grand Rapids: Radio Bible Class, 1973.

Fackre, Gabriel. *The Religious Right and Christian Faith.* Grand Rapids: Eerdmans, 1982.

Falwell, Jerry. *Listen, America!* 1980. New York: Bantam, 1981.

Falwell, Jerry, ed., with Ed Dobson and Ed Hindson. *The Fundamentalist Phenomenon: The Resurgence of Conservative Christianity.* Garden City: Galilee-Doubleday, 1981.

Farah, Charles. "America's Pentecostals: What They Believe." *Christianity Today* 16 Oct. 1987: 22–26.

Fish, Stanley. *Is There a Text in This Class? The Authority of Interpretive Communities.* Cambridge: Harvard UP, 1980. This is a collection of critical essays, some of which first appeared in print elsewhere: "Interpreting the *Variorum*" (147–73), *Critical Inquiry* 2 (1976). "Normal Circumstances and Other Special Cases" (268–92), *Critical Inquiry* 4 (1978). "A Reply to John Reichert" (293–99), *Critical Inquiry* 5 (1979). "Is There a Text in This Class?" (303–21) and "What Makes an Interpretation Acceptable?" (338–55) were originally delivered as the John Crowe Ransom Memorial Lectures at Kenyon College, 8–13 April 1979.

Fitzgerald, Frances. "A Disciplined, Charging Army." *The New Yorker* 18 May 1981: 53–141.

Foucault, Michel. *The Archaeology of Knowledge.* Trans. A.M. Sheridan Smith. London: Tavistock, 1972. New York: Pantheon-Random, 1972. Trans. of *L'Archéologie du Savoir.* Paris: Gallimard, 1969.
———*The Discourse on Language.* Trans. Rupert Swyer. Foucault, *Archaeology* 215–237. Trans. of *L'ordre du discours.* Paris: Gallimard, 1971.
———*The Foucault Reader.* Ed. Paul Rabinow. New York: Pantheon-Random, 1984.
———"Space, Knowledge, and Power." Interview. Trans. Christian Hubert. *Foucault Reader* 239–56.
———"The Subject and Power." Afterword. *Michel Foucault: Beyond Structuralism and Hermeneutics.* By Hubert L. Dreyfus and Paul Rabinow. Chicago: U of Chicago P, 1982. 208–26. This article is in two parts: "Why Study Power: The Question of the Subject" (208–16) was written in English by Foucault; "How is Power Exercised" (216–26) trans. Leslie Sawyer.
———"Truth and Power." Interview. *Foucault Reader* 51–75.

Frame, Randy. "Battle on the Bible." *Christianity Today* 12 June 1987: 44–46.
———"Inerrancy Council Searches for Unity on Tough Issues." *Christianity Today* 6 Feb. 1987: 38–39.

Frei, Hans W. *The Eclipse of Biblical Narrative: A Study in Eighteenth and Nineteenth Century Hermeneutics.* New Haven: Yale UP, 1974.

Geisler, Norman L., ed. *Inerrancy.* Grand Rapids: Zondervan, 1979.

Graff, Gerald. "The Pseudo-Politics of Interpretation." *Critical Inquiry* 9 (1983): 597–610.

Gritsch, Eric W. *Born Againism: Perspectives on a Movement.* Philadelphia: Fortress, 1982.

Greene, Oliver B. *The Second Coming of Jesus.* Greenville: Gospel Hour, 1971.

Hahn, Jessica. Interview. *Playboy* Nov. 1987: 82+.

Handelman, Susan A. *The Slayers of Moses: The Emergence of Rabbinic Interpretation in Modern Literary Theory.* Albany: State U of New York P, 1982.

Hatch, Nathan O. and Mark A. Noll, eds. *The Bible in America: Essays in Cultural History.* New York: Oxford UP, 1982.

Hatch, Nathan O. "Sola Scriptura and Novus Ordo Seclorum." Hatch and Noll 59–78.

Henry, Carl F. H. *God, Revelation and Authority.* Vol. 4. Waco: Word Books, 1979.

Hirsch. E. D., Jr. *The Aims of Interpretation.* Chicago: U of Chicago P, 1976.
———"The Politics of Theories of Interpretation." *Critical Inquiry* 9 (1982): 235–47.
———*Validity in Interpretation.* New Haven: Yale UP, 1967.

Hodge, Charles. *Systematic Theology.* Vol. 1. New York: Scribner, Armstrong, 1873.

Hofstadter, Richard. *Anti-intellectualism in American Life.* New York: Knopf, 1962.

Hunter, James Davison. *Evangelicalism: The Coming Generation.* Chicago: U of Chicago P, 1987.

Hutson, Curtis. "The Value of a Soul." *Sword of the Lord.* 3 July 1981: 1+.

Hyles, Jack. *The Hyles Visitation Manual.* Hammond, IN: Hyles-Anderson, 1975.

Johnston, Robert K., ed. *The Use of the Bible in Theology: Evangelical Options.* Atlanta: John Knox P, 1985.

Jones, Bob. Editorial. *Faith for the Family.* July/August 1978: [5.]

Kaiser, Walter C., Jr. "Legitimate Hermeneutics." Geisler 117–47.

Kantzer, Kenneth S. "Troublesome Questions." *Christianity Today* 20 March 1987: 45.

Kermode, Frank. "Can We Say Absolutely Anything We Like? *Art, Politics, and Will: Essays in Honor of Lionel Trilling.* Ed. Quentin Anderson, et al. New York: Basic, 1977. 159–72.
———*The Genesis of Secrecy: On the Interpretation of Narrative.* Cambridge: Harvard UP, 1979.

LaHaye, Tim. *The Battle for the Mind.* Old Tappan, NJ: Power-Revell, 1980.

Liberty Commentary on the New Testament. Exec. Ed., Jerry Falwell. Lynchburg, VA: Liberty P, 1978.

Lindsell, Harold. *The Battle for the Bible*. Grand Rapids: Zondervan, 1976.
———*The World, the Flesh, and the Devil*. "Special Crusade Edition." Minneapolis: World Wide Publications, 1973. "Published for the Billy Graham Evangelistic Association."

Lindsey, Hal. *The Late Great Planet Earth*. Grand Rapids: Zondervan, 1970.

Lundin, Roger. "Our Hermeneutical Inheritance." *The Responsibility of Hermeneutics*. By Lundin, et al. Exeter, Paternoster; Grand Rapids, Eerdmans, 1985. 1–29.

Machen, J. Gresham. *Christianity and Liberalism*. 1923. Grand Rapids: Eerdmans, 1946.

Marsden, George. *Fundamentalism and American Culture: The Shaping of Twentieth-Century Evangelicalism: 1870–1925*. New York: Oxford UP, 1980.

Marty, Martin E. "Fundamentalism Reborn." *Saturday Review* May 1980: 37–42.
———*Religion and Republic: The American Circumstance*. Boston: Beacon, 1987.

Mencken, H. L. *Treatise on the Gods*. New York: Knopf, 1930.

Mumford, Bob. *Take Another Look at Guidance: A Study of Divine Guidance*. Plainfield, NJ: Logos International, 1971.

Neff, David. "The Down Side of Civility." *Christianity Today* 6 Feb. 1987: 13.

The New Scofield Reference Bible. New York: Oxford UP, 1967.

Nicole, Roger. "Universalism: Will Everyone Be Saved?" *Christianity Today* 20 March 1987: 32–39.

Noll, Mark A. "Evangelicals and the Study of the Bible." *Evangelicalism and Modern America*. Ed. George Marsden. Grand Rapids: Eerdmans, 1984. 103–21.

Orfitelli, Lonnie. "My Search." *Decision* Sept. 1986: 4–5. *Decision* is published by the Billy Graham Evangelistic Association.

"Our Future Hope: Eschatology and Its Role in the Church." A Christianity Today Institute symposium. *Christianity Today* 6 Feb. 1987: 1–I through 14–I. Participants were: John Walvoord, Gleason Archer, Alan F. Johnson, Anthony Hoekema, John Jefferson Davis, and Kenneth S. Kantzer.

Packer, J. I. *"Fundamentalism" and the Word of God: Some Evangelical Principles*. 1958. Grand Rapids: Eerdmans, 1974.
———"In Quest of Canonical Interpretation." Johnston 35–55.

Paine, Stephen W. Interview. *Houghton Milieu* Winter 1978: 1–3. (The Houghton Milieu is the alumni magazine of Houghton College, an evangelical college in Houghton, New York, of which Paine is past president.)

Payne, J. Barton. "Higher Criticism and Biblical Inerrancy." Geisler 85–113.

Peshkin, Alan. *God's Choice: The Total World of a Fundamentalist Christian School.* Chicago: U of Chicago P, 1986.

Piepkorn, Arthur Carl. "What Does 'Inerrancy' Mean?" *Concordia Theological Monthly* 36 (1965): 577–93.

Pingry, Patricia. *Jerry Falwell: Man of Vision.* Milwaukee: Ideals, 1980.

Pinnock, Clark. "Fire, Then Nothing." *Christianity Today* 20 March 1987: 40–41.
————"How I Use the Bible in Doing Theology." Johnston 18–34.
————" '...This Treasure in Earthen Vessels': The Inspiration and Interpretation of the Bible." *Sojourners* Oct. 1980: 16–19.

Punt, Neal. "All Are Saved Except." *Christianity Today* 20 March 1987: 43–44.

Pyle, Hugh F. "One More Night with the Frogs." *Sword of the Lord* 29 May 1981: 1+.

"Reagan Defends Use of Scripture." *Washington Post* 22 Feb. 1985: A14.

Rice, John R. *Dr. Rice, Here Are More Questions...* Vol. 2. Murfreesboro, Tenn.: Sword of the Lord, 1973. This collection is a compilation of material originally appearing in Rice's weekly tabloid *The Sword of the Lord.*

Robertson, Pat. *Answers to 200 of Life's Most Probing Questions.* Virginia Beach: Christian Broadcasting Network, 1984.

"The Root of the Problem." *The F. A. Newsletter* 2.2 (June 1986): 3. This newsletter is published by Fundamentalists Anonymous, P.O. Box 20324, Greeley Square Station, New York, New York 10001.

Ryle, J. C. "No More Crying! A Sermon to Children." *The Sword of the Lord* 26 June 1981: 3+.

Said, Edward W. *Beginnings: Intention and Method.* New York: Basic, 1975.
————"Opponents, Audiences, Constituencies, and Community." *Critical Inquiry* 9 (1982): 1–26.
————*The World, the Text, and the Critic.* Cambridge: Harvard UP, 1983.

Sandeen, Ernest. *The Roots of Fundamentalism: British and American Millenarianism, 1800–1930.* Chicago: U of Chicago P, 1970.

Schaeffer, Francis A. *The God Who Is There.* Downers Grove, IL: Inter-Varsity, 1968.
————*No Final Conflict: The Bible Without Error in All That It Affirms.* Downers Grove, IL: Inter-Varsity, 1975.

Schneidau, Herbert N. *Sacred Discontent: The Bible and Western Tradition.* Baton Rouge: Louisiana State UP, 1976.

Scofield, C.I. *Rightly Dividing the Word of Truth.* New York: Gospel Publishing House, n.d.
————*What Do the Prophets Say?* 1918. Greenville: Gospel Hour, n.d.

Scofield Reference Bible. 2nd Ed. New York: Oxford UP, 1945. This is the 1917 edition; the first edition appeared in 1909.

Sellers, C. Norman. *Biblical Conclusions Concerning Tongues*. Miami: n.p., 1972.

Stevick, Daniel B. *Beyond Fundamentalism*. Richmond: John Knox, 1964.

Stout, Harry S. "Word and Order in Colonial New England." Hatch and Noll 19–38.

Streiker, Lowell D. *The Gospel Time Bomb: Ultrafundamentalism and the Future of America*. Buffalo: Prometheus, 1984.

Swaggart, Jimmy. "Pentecostals and Charismatics." *The Evangelist* July 1987: 4–9.

Tarr, Leslie K. "The Hermetically-Sealed World of Neo-Fundamentalism." *Eternity* Aug. 1976: 24+.

Taylor, Robert G., Jr. "The Horrible Pit." *Prize Winning Evangelistic Sermons*. Comp. and Ed. John R. Rice. Murfreesboro, TN: Sword of the Lord, 1976. 73–86. (This is a collection of the top ten sermons in *The Sword of the Lord*'s 1976 evangelistic sermon contest.)

Tillich, Paul. *Biblical Religion and the Search for Ultimate Reality*. Chicago: U of Chicago P, 1955.

Torrey, R.A. *Difficulties and Alleged Errors and Contradictions in the Bible*. Chicago: Bible Institute Colportage Association, 1907.

Towns, Elmer and Jerry Falwell. *Church Aflame*. Nashville: Impact Books, 1971.

Trinity Baptist College, Jacksonville, FL. Advertisement. *The Sword of the Lord* 5 June 1981: 7.

Twain, Mark. "Letters from the Earth." *Letters from the Earth*. 1942. Ed. Bernard DeVoto. New York: Perennial-Harper and Row, 1974. 11–55. "Letters from the Earth" was written c. 1909.

Van Gorder, Paul P. "The Pastor as Leader." Wiersbe, et al. 19–30.

van Impe, Jack. *Signs of the Times*. Clawson, MI: Jack van Impe Ministries, 1979.

Warfield, Benjamin Breckenridge. "The Inspiration of the Bible." *Bibliotecha Sacra* 51 (1894): 614–40. Rpt. in *Revelation and Inspiration* 51–74.
———"Inspiration and Criticism." Address. Western Theological Seminary. N.d. [c. 1878.] Rpt. in *Revelation and Inspiration* 395–425.
———*Revelation and Inspiration*. New York: Oxford UP, 1927.

Weber, Timothy P. *Living in the Shadow of the Second Coming: American Premillennialism, 1875–1982*. Grand Rapids: Academic-Zondervan, 1983.
———"The Two-Edged Sword: The Fundamentalist Use of the Bible." Hatch and Noll 101–20.

Wells, David F. "Everlasting Punishment." *Christianity Today* 20 March 1987: 41–42.

Wiersbe, Warren W. "The Pastor as Preacher." Wiersbe, et al. 3–16.

Wiersbe, Warren W., Paul R. Van Gorder, and Howard F. Sugden. *Priorities for the Pastor*. 1980. Grand Rapids, Baker, 1982. The 1980 copyright is held by Radio Bible Class; the book was first published under the title *Person to Parson*.

Wilkerson, David. "Last-Day Witnesses!" *The Evangelist* Oct. 1987: 13–16.

Young, Perry Deane. *God's Bullies: Native Reflections on Preachers and Politics.* New York: Holt, 1982.

Index

Authority: of biblical text, 1–15, 107–09; of Christ and his teachings, 12, 32–34, 51–52; of commentary, 78–82, 84; of Holy Spirit, 14, 28, 35–36, 78, 87–88, 92–94; of institutions, 18, 82–84; of interpretive community, 19–22, 61–75, 83; of original autographs, 29–35, 62; of personal experience, 80, 92–95; of preachers and pastors, 2, 14–15, 85–92, 95–98, 109, 111, 113–14; of translations, 27, 29, 31–34, 48. *See also* Inerrancy; Literalism

Archer, Gleason L., 24–25, 72, 73

Armstrong, Herbert W., 65

Bahnsen, Greg L., 34

Bakker, Jim, 57, 96–97, 110, 113–14

Barnhart, Joe Edward, 24, 57–58, 82, 105, 115n, 120n, 121n, 124n

Barr, James, 3, 8, 9, 10, 34, 44–45, 46, 52, 68, 72, 82, 108, 116n, 117n, 118n, 121n, 122–23n, 127n

Bates, Leon I., 42–43

Beegle, Dewey, 26, 34, 35, 68, 73, 79, 116n, 117n, 120n

Bible, interpretation of: fundamentalist compared to mainline Prostestant, 18, 25; relation to literary theory and interpretation, 1–2, 12, 17–22, 27–28, 30, 36, 39, 47, 48–49, 50, 65, 66, 71, 108; source criticism, 32, 45, 47. *See also* Fundamentalism; Inerrancy; Literalism

Biblical inerrancy. *See* Inerrancy

Bloesch, Donald G., 122n

Born Again (PBS documentary), 90–93, 101, 123n

Bultmann, Rudolf, 28

Burke, Kenneth, 118n

Charismatics and Pentecostals, 7–8, 10, 36, 116n. *See also* Fundamentalism, definition of "Chicago Statement on Biblical Inerrancy, The", 26, 29, 30, 33

Christensen, Larry, 124n

Christianity Today, 8, 53, 72, 104–05, 127n

Ciardi, John, 27

Costen, Elaine, 86

Culler, Jonathan, 127n

Darby, J. N., 40

Dayton, Donald, 116n

Decision, 116n

DeHaan, Richard W., 12, 57, 87, 88, 95, 124n

Derrida, Jacques, 67

Dictation, 32, 117–18n. *See also* Authority, of Holy Spirit; Inspiration

Dispensationalism, 13, 40, 50–55, 79–81, 89, 118n, 119n, 123n. *See also* Premillennialism

Evangelist, The, 126n

Fackre, Gabriel, 18, 121n

Falwell, Jerry, 6, 57, 59–60, 79, 84, 85–86, 90, 95–97, 113–14, 115–16n, 118n, 126n

Farah, Charles, 116n

Fish, Stanley, 1, 19–20, 48–49, 61–62, 65, 67, 70, 73, 74–75, 110, 120n, 122n

Fitzgerald, Frances, 84, 94

Foucault, Michel, 1–2, 14, 48, 58, 64, 67, 75, 78, 82, 84, 96, 107, 109–10, 127n

Frei, Hans, 46–47, 49–50, 117–18n, 121n

Friedman, Robert I., 120n

Fundamentalism, 1–4; definition of, 5–15,
115n, 117n, 118n; relation to
Evangelicalism, 8–11, 115n, 116n, 118n,
120n. *See also* Authority; Bible, interpretation of; Inerrancy; Literalism
Fundamentalists Anonymous, 7

Graff, Gerald, 121n
Graham, Billy, 8, 115n
Greene, Oliver B., 40–42, 44, 87–88
Gritsch, Eric, 18, 25, 118n

Hahn, Jessica, 84
Handelman, Susan, 49
Hatch, Nathan, 64
Hell, doctrine of, 47, 99–106
Henry, Carl F. H., 9, 28–29, 39, 72, 122n,
122–23n
Hirsch, E. D., 19–20, 28, 65–68, 121n,
122n
Hodge, Charles, 11, 17, 30, 55–56, 66,
116n
Hoekema, Anthony, 72
Hofstadter, Richard, 6
Humbard, Rex, 57
Hunter, James Davidson, 8, 23, 103–04,
116n, 124n
Hutson, Curtis, 100
Hyles, Jack, 102–03

Inerrancy, 13, 19, 23–37, 61–62, 68,
72–75, 95, 107–09, 111, 117n, 118n,
120n, 121n, 123n; in relation to
literalism, 44–49. *See also* Authority
Ingersoll, Robert, 73
Inspiration, 25–26, 31–32, 117–18n. *See
also* Authority, of Holy Spirit; Dictation
International Conference on Biblical Inerrancy (1978), 11–12, 26
Interpretive community. *See* Authority, of
interpretive community; Fish, Stanley

Jehovah's Witnesses, 65
Johnston, Robert K., 9
Jones, Bob, 53–54

Kaiser, Walter C., Jr., 119n, 122n
Kantzer, Kenneth, 104–06

Kermode, Frank, 17, 18, 49, 55, 80, 108,
127n
King James Version, 32, 40, 123n

LaHaye, Tim, 58–59
Lindsell, Harold, 12, 19, 24, 29–30, 45–46,
73–74, 82, 117n, 121n, 124–25n
Lindsey, Hal, 42–43, 55–56, 120n
Literalism, 13, 39–60, 95, 121n; conflicts
with inerrancy, 44–49; hostility to
figural interpretations, 45–47; literal interpretations of eschatological passages,
40–44, 52–56, 71–72; literal interpretations of Genesis, 45–46, 62–63; literal interpretations of hellfire, 47, 99–106. *See
also* Dispensationalism.
Literary theory and interpretation. *See*
Bible, interpretation of, relation to
literary theory and interpretation
Lundin, Roger, 122n

Machen, J. Gresham, 23, 57, 72, 89, 99
Marsden, George, 3, 74, 117n, 118n, 119n,
120n
Marty, Martin, 6
Mencken, H. L., 65
Moody, Dwight L., 6, 11
Mumford, Bob, 93–94

New International Version, 32, 48
New Scofield Reference Bible, 13–14, 32,
40, 55, 63, 79–80, 117n, 119n. *See also
Scofield Reference Bible*
Nicole, Roger, 105
Noll, Mark A., 74, 124n

Odle, Joe T., 84
Orfitelli, Lonnie, 116n

Packer, J. I., 8, 29, 31, 33, 35–36, 70–72,
75, 95, 117n, 118n, 119n
Paine, Stephen W., 48
Paisley, Ian, 115n
Patterson, Ben, 127n
Paul, Saint, 24, 47, 51, 53
Payne, J. Barton, 74
Peshkin, Alan, 6, 9, 54, 59, 83, 85, 88, 93,
100, 101, 115n, 123n, 124n, 125n